MARRIAGE
RESPICED

Rediscovering God's Blueprint for Love, Covenant and Intimacy

By Sharon M Finney

Copyright © 2025 by Sharon M Finney

All rights reserved.

No portion of this book may be reproduced in any form without written permission from the publisher or author, except as permitted by U.S. copyright law.

Contents

Forward	V
Preface	VIII
Acknowledgements	XI
1. Marriages Divine Plan	1
2. Building a Christ-Centered Marriage	11
3. Men & Women - God's Design Appreciating the Differences Between the Two	19
4. Communication as the Cornerstone	32
5. Building Emotional Intimacy	45
6. Navigating Conflict with Grace	51
7. Physical Intimacy and Connection	61
8. Financial Harmony in Marriage	79
9. Balancing Individuality and Shared Goals	88
10. Trust and Forgiveness	99
11. Familial and Social Influences	111
12. Cultivating Self-Awareness in Marriage	118
Conclusion	126
References	129

Nuggets	131
Covenant Commitment Statement	133
A Final Word	134
About the Author	135

Forward

Marriage is one of God's most sacred gifts, but it also presents some of the biggest challenges found in human relationships. It is often misunderstood, causing many marriages to end in divorce. This sacred union is both a covenant and a calling, a refuge and a refining fire. Over the years, I have had the privilege of walking with hundreds of couples as a pastor and marriage and family therapist, listening to their hopes, sharing their pain, and helping them rediscover the purpose and promise within their union. I have personally seen, in my own marriage and in those I have been privileged to walk with, a simple yet profound truth: marriages grow not just through technique but through transformation—transformation rooted in Christ.

It is from this place that I wholeheartedly commend this book to you.

Sharon Finney is not only a dear friend but also someone who once served as my clinical supervisor during my training as a marriage and family therapist. I have learned from her wisdom, integrity, and strong commitment to both clinical excellence and spiritual faithfulness. She is an experienced Licensed Marriage and Family Therapist (LMFT) who has guided many couples through the complex, often messy reality of marriage. Equally important, she is a devoted follower of Jesus Christ who understands that spiritual growth and relational health are deeply connected.

This book does not view marriage as a contract to manage, but as a sacred covenant to steward—one meant to reflect God's love, grace, and faithfulness. It speaks clearly and compassionately to common issues couples face: communication problems, unresolved conflicts, financial worries, unmet expectations, and emotional distance. Still, it remains rooted in the deeper spiritual foundation that nurtures lasting marital health.

What makes this work especially compelling is its blend of sound therapeutic insights with deep theological grounding. Instead of providing quick fixes or superficial solutions, Sharon encourages couples to embark on a more meaningful journey—one that requires commitment, intentional growth, and mutual submission to Christ. She recognizes that when couples learn to grow together spiritually, communicate with humility, face problems as partners rather than enemies, and center their lives around God's purposes, peace becomes achievable—not because conflict vanishes, but because love matures.

After pastoring for nearly twenty years, I can confirm the urgent need for resources like this book. Too often, couples must choose between faith-based guidance that lacks clinical depth and therapeutic options that neglect spiritual truth. <u>Marriage Respiced</u> bridges that gap with grace and wisdom. It respects the complexity of human relationships while grounding marriage in the redemptive love of God.

Whether you are newly married, preparing to get married, going through a tough time, or just looking to strengthen an already healthy relationship, this book provides both hope and guidance. It is pastoral without being overly sentimental, scholarly but accessible, and deeply spiritual while still recognizing the practical aspects of daily life.

Marriage, at its best, reflects God's love. My prayer is that as you read these pages, you will be encouraged not only to strengthen your marriage but also to deepen your relationship with Christ.

— Rev. Byron L. Benton, PhD, MDiv

Preface

A FEW YEARS AGO, I sat across from a couple in distress. Their eyes conveyed stories of forgotten dreams and lost love. They are not by themselves. Many couples are caught in a vicious cycle of disagreements and miscommunications. However, they yearn for the happiness and tranquility that come with marriage. The story of this couple is not unique but highlights a reality that is often overlooked. God's love and commitment to us are reflected in marriage, which is a sacred journey.

Today, many marriages face challenges that seem insurmountable. We live in a world that often reduces marriage to a mere contract. Divorce rates are high, and many couples feel overwhelmed. They struggle with communication, intimacy, and balancing responsibilities. The importance of returning to God's original design for marriage is more urgent than ever. Statistics show that couples who have a spiritual perspective on marriage report greater longevity and levels of satisfaction.

The goal of this book is to help couples develop a marriage centered on Christ, that is full of intimacy and exploration. It is based on covenant, love, and dedication. These components provide the capacity to improve and change marital relationships. There are practical, spiritual, and emotional advantages to viewing marriage from a sacred perspective. Couples who adopt this perspective experience greater intimacy, improved communication, and increased fortitude in the face of adversity.

The inspiration for this book comes from the rich symbolism of the Jewish wedding feast. In Jewish tradition, a wedding is not just a celebration. It is a covenant, a sacred promise reflecting God's unwavering love. This perspective enriches our understanding of marriage as more than a contract. It is a divine commitment, a reflection of the relationship between Christ and the Church.

Throughout this book, we will explore key themes essential for a thriving marriage. We will discuss communication, intimacy, financial harmony, and resilience. These themes provide a roadmap for what you can expect to learn. They are designed to equip you with tools to nurture a Christ-centered union.

Let me share a bit about my background. I am a Licensed Marriage and Family Therapist. My passion is helping couples achieve a lasting, Christ-centered marriage. Over the years, I have counseled many couples, guiding them through challenges, observing the transformation of those with a foundation of faith and those without. I have seen firsthand the transformative power of a sacred marriage perspective. My professional work and personal experiences have equipped me to offer practical and spiritual guidance to strengthen the marital relationship and stoke the fires of passion to keep them burning hot.

As we journey together through this book, I invite you to view your marriage through the lens of divine purpose and commitment. Let us explore how a sacred marriage can reflect God's love and grace. I encourage you to embark on this transformative journey, allowing your marriage to be nourished for every season of life, rooted in faith and love.

The foundation of this book lies in understanding marriage as a divine institution. It is not just a human arrangement. God's vision for marriage includes love, companionship, and purpose. It reflects His passion and commitment to His people.

A solid marriage is built on prayer. Spiritual unity is strengthened when couples pray together. It helps face obstacles with grace and brings God into the relationship.

God's unending love for people is reflected in marriage, a divine institution. When God first established marriage, He said, "It is not good for the man to be alone." I will make him a helper suitable for him. (Genesis 2:18 NIV). This statement emphasizes that companionship is the foundation of marriage and reflects God's recognition for camaraderie. God's plan for marriage remains unchanged, despite societal views and the challenges that couples now face. It is crucial to return to the Creator's original plan during trying times, which is a sacred covenant that reflects His dedication, love, and grace.

Marriage is a reflection of Christ's relationship with His bride, the Church, as Scripture affirms in Ephesians 5:25-32. Couples can experience a renewed sense of fulfillment, joy, and purpose in their relationship by embracing this truth. The foundation of enduring marital love is God's covenant love, which is unfailing and selfless in nature.

Acknowledgements

I AM DEEPLY GRATEFUL to the many people who have supported me throughout this journey and made this book possible.

First and foremost, I extend my heartfelt thanks to my committed prayer team who continuously hold my arms up and cover me in prayer. Your faithful intercession has been a source of strength and encouragement that has carried me through every challenge and triumph.

To Gwen Benton, who has been a remarkable accountability partner and tireless editor—your dedication, keen eye for detail, and unwavering support have been invaluable. This book is immeasurably better because of your contributions and partnership.

To my son Martinez, thank you for teaching me the process of composing and publishing my books. Your patience, expertise, and willingness to share your knowledge have empowered me to bring my vision to life. I am grateful not only for your technical guidance but for believing in this project.

To my son Marquis, thank you for managing the business side of my endeavors and for encouraging me to keep pushing forward when the path seemed uncertain. Your leadership and constant encouragement have been instrumental in making this dream a reality.

Each of you has played a vital role in this accomplishment, and I am forever grateful for your investment in me and in this work. May God bless you abundantly as you have blessed me.

Chapter 1

Marriages Divine Plan

A COUPLE SHARED THEIR story of pain and uncertainty with me. Unfortunately, the marriage no longer felt like the happy union they had dreamed of; it felt more like a weary obligation, marked by complaints and responsibility. Daily misunderstandings clouded their relationship, and the spark had diminished. They were desperate for change and wanted to learn how to restore what they had lost. Over time they reinterpreted their relationship through the prism of divine love and dedication. They began to view their union as a sacred covenant that mirrored the bond between God and man, rather than just a contract. This change gave their marriage new meaning and happiness, which resulted in a closer bond and a greater level of fulfillment than they had ever dreamed.

Marriage today faces numerous difficulties; it is often viewed as a contract that can be readily broken when convenience dictates it. The original purpose of this holy institution has been obscured by changing societal perceptions. Couples face many challenges and temptations, ranging from internal issues such as communication barriers to external pressures like job demands. But recognizing marriage as God intended it to be provides a way to find contentment and harmony again. The divine origin of marriage is profoundly revealed by the creation story in Genesis, which shows its purpose as a harmonious partnership that reflects divine love and unity (Turpin, 2016).

God's original plan for marriage is revealed in Genesis. Adam and Eve were created to be companions and share in the joys and challenges of life. This story lays the groundwork for marriage as an expression of God's unity and love. It is an illustration of how two people united together as one, "bone of my bone flesh of my flesh" that cannot be separated. This oneness extends beyond the physical union, encompassing spiritual, intellectual, and emotional aspects, which creates a profound bond. God's character is reflected in this unity, thus emphasizing love, harmony, and support for one another. To reflect God's love for creation, marriage becomes a living example of His image.

Balanced spiritual leadership and collaboration are also necessary for a happy marriage. Scripture describes roles for husbands and wives that encourage mutual respect and growth. Following Christ's example, the husband is expected to lead with humility and love. The wife participates in this spiritual journey by following the wisdom and guidance of her husband while providing support along the way. Together, they establish

a relationship that glorifies God and fosters the family's spiritual development. The relationship becomes a collaboration with God.

One Flesh: A Reflection of God's Unity

"The two will become one flesh," according to the Bible (Genesis 2:24 KJV). This includes spiritual, intellectual, and emotional unity in addition to physical unity. The union of the Father, Son, and Holy Spirit, who are separate but inseparable, is represented by the marriage bond. The closer you become to God, the more intimacy you experience with Him. The deeper you go, the more you experience the revelation of who He is in every aspect of your being. We are the bride, and Christ is the husbandman. Intimacy with Jesus and intimacy with your spouse are so intertwined in the heart of God that He established both with a blood covenant. Paul quotes Genesis 2:24 in Ephesians 5:31-32 and says, "This is a profound mystery, but I am talking about Christ and the Church."(NIV)

Marriage is more than a partnership; it is a profound reflection of God's relationship with humanity. The story of Hosea and Gomer serves as an example of this divine metaphor. As a living example of God's loyalty to Israel despite its adultery, God gave the prophet Hosea instructions to wed the unfaithful Gomer. This story emphasizes a love that endures despite hardship and betrayal. It is a potent reminder that marriage necessitates unwavering love and dedication, just like God's covenant with His people. Hosea's commitment encourages spouses to view their union as a holy representation of divine love that transcends all circumstances. However, this story does not provide a license for infidelity.

Marriage between a man and his wife is a spiritual metaphor of Christ and the Church. Spouses are expected to love one another sincerely and faithfully, just as Christ loves the Church with an unending love. This illustration encourages couples to see their relationship through the eyes of Heaven, elevating marriage from a simple earthly contract to a heavenly covenant. Couples can build a marriage that reflects the divine bond between Christ and His Bride by spiritual growth and mutual commitment. This viewpoint strengthens the marriage by transforming everyday encounters into opportunities to exercise kindness and grace.

Seeing every day as a gift and encouraging spiritual development together are key components of developing a heavenly perspective in a marriage. The foundation of this divine perspective is the practice of appreciation and thankfulness. The atmosphere at home can be changed with a simple "thank you" or acknowledgement of each other's efforts. The relationship can be anchored in faith by promoting spiritual activities such as scripture reading or praying together as a couple. Establishing prayer as a foundational principle helps couples navigate difficulties together by bringing divine strength and direction into the union. It further provides a place to return to when direction has been lost.

Pursuing holiness together is a vital aspect of reflecting God's image in marriage. By participating in Bible study, prayer, praise and worship together, and daily practice of Christian virtues, couples develop a greater sense of oneness. A supernatural ambiance is created in the home when a couple sets aside time to participate in worship and praise (thanksgiving). Studying the Bible together improves comprehension and fosters spiritual discussion, both of which contribute to a stronger more fulfilling marriage. Couples demonstrate God's purity in their actions by resolving to live out virtues such as kindness, patience, and humility. Because of this quest for morality, marriage becomes a daily act of worship, in which both partners support and aid each other on their spiritual path.

Intentionality and commitment are necessary for marriage to reflect God's image. To embody the divine relationship it represents, it requires daily acts of grace, forgiveness, and love. Couples can make their marriage a symbol of God's unwavering love and devotion. When the mindset becomes that all things are done for the glory of God, every interaction, from quiet times of introspection to shared laughter, reflects His divine love.

Couples grow closer to God and to one another by fostering a holy union. Marriage becomes a tangible manifestation of His faithfulness and love, thus encouraging others to pursue the same level of intimacy in their own relationships. Couples forge a legacy of love that embodies the divine image they are called to as they develop spiritually together.

Marriage becomes a reflection of the ultimate union between Christ and His Church through these customs, transcending its earthly limitations. To create a marriage that genuinely reflects God's image and love for people, this sacred perspective encourages couples to engage deeply with both their faith and with one another.

The Symbolism of the Jewish Wedding Feast

Jewish wedding customs offer a rich tapestry of customs, each with enduring significance and deep meaning. These traditions provide valuable insights for modern Christian marriages, highlighting the commitment and spiritual depth of the marital union. The betrothal process, a time of promise and preparation, is a key component in understanding the value of covenant and commitment. While living separately, the couple is legally bound during this time, signifying a commitment similar to an engagement but with more profound covenantal implications. This period emphasizes the seriousness of marriage and ensures that both people are emotionally and spiritually ready for the lifelong commitment they are about to make.

Another essential component of Jewish wedding ceremonies is the chuppah (wedding canopy). It represents the house the couple will construct together, which will be open on all sides to receive family and friends. Vows are exchanged under this canopy as an expression of the couple's desire to build a life together based on respect and love. This aspect of the ceremony is not just a formality but a potent ritual that sanctifies the union. It is a symbol of hospitality and a reminder to the couple that their union is supported by the community. This communal element promotes a sense of belonging and shared responsibility by encouraging the couple to seek advice and support from their loved ones.

The wedding feast represents joy and commitment. It honors the joining of families and communities through the union of two people. The significance of wine in this celebration cannot be overstated; it stands for joy, abundance, and the deep satisfaction that comes from this holy union. In many ceremonies, the couple shares wine as a symbol of their future together with all of its challenges and sweetness. The group celebration highlights that love flourishes in community and reaffirms that marriage is a covenant upheld by those surrounding the couple.

Deep insights into the spiritual aspects of marriage can be gained by drawing comparisons between the Marriage Supper of the Lamb and the Jewish wedding feast. Christians look forward to Christ's return and their final union with Him, just as a Jewish couple looks forward to their wedding day. This hope for the future highlights the temporal aspect of marriage while emphasizing its timeless value as an expression of divine love. The Marriage Supper of the Lamb invites us to consider our earthly marriages as a preview of that celestial feast symbolizing the happy conclusion of history where Christ and His Church are joined together forever.

Modern couples can learn important lessons from Jewish customs to improve their own marriages. One lesson is the importance of community support; marriage involves a network of family and friends who offer support and direction. Anniversaries and vow renewals are examples of celebration and remembrance rituals that help couples commemorate their shared past and reaffirm their future commitments. These memories cultivate gratitude and help couples focus on the unwavering love that sustains them through life's highs and lows.

Imagine a couple who chooses to apply these practices to their lives by inviting close friends and family to join them for an anniversary dinner every year. They reminisce about the struggles and victories of their marriage throughout the past year. By reminding them that they are not on this journey alone, this ritual not only deepens their relationship but also fortifies their support system.

Rituals: Reflection and Remembrance

Reflect on rituals or traditions you can create or implement in your marriage to commemorate significant occasions or strengthen your relationship. Consider how you can invite your community to be a part of these festivities, fostering opportunities for mutual happiness and encouragement. As life's special moments occur, celebrating them with personalized intentionality gives them meaning. Discuss these concepts with your spouse and make plans for special ways to commemorate your journey together.

Highlighting your journey of development and transformation serves as a reminder of how far you have come. On an occasion such as your anniversary, writing and exchanging vows strengthen the bonds that unite you and renew your commitment to one another. Intimate rituals transform these days into heartfelt displays of affection, leaving lasting memories that endure long after the day is over.

Simple rituals can have a significant impact. Lighting a candle during dinner to mark the end of the day's distractions and the transition into a time of unity or saying a short prayer to release the stresses of the day and focus on one another allows moments to reflect. To further strengthen the relationship, designate time each week for open conversations to reflect on the successes and areas of improvement implemented and needed from your past week.

Traditional Jewish wedding customs emphasize the value of rituals in strengthening the bonds between spouses. Couples can be inspired by these practices to embody the sacred covenant of love bolstered by community support and rooted in unwavering commitment.

Understanding Covenant Love

Beyond the temporary nature of feelings and the shallowness of simple agreements, covenant love is a profound and enduring commitment. Covenant love is an unwavering commitment at the core of marriage, supporting both partners through challenges and successes. Unlike ordinary love, it focuses on appreciating each spouse for who they are, ensuring stability and fostering an environment where both can grow. Agape, or divine, selfless, and unconditional love, is what covenant love is.

Contractual agreements in marriages, as opposed to covenant love, often depend on specific terms and reciprocal benefits. Contracts are typically created with certain conditions and expectations, and they can be terminated if those expectations are not fulfilled. Covenant love, however, is restrained by restrictions or conditions. It emphasizes a lifetime commitment of longevity and faithfulness. as reflected in God's unwavering promise to Noah and His covenant with Abraham. These covenants emphasize the qualities of an unbreakable bond for which marriages should strive.

It takes commitment and intentionality to live out covenant love. It involves making decisions every day that demonstrate dedication to one another. Simple deeds of kindness, such as writing a supportive note or cooking a favorite meal, strengthen ties of love and gratitude. These daily reminders initiate a positive feedback loop of love and appreciation that improves the relationship and reinforces the commitment to continuous relational development. These thoughtful acts of kindness encourage both partners to grow together and adapt as necessary to life's changes.

Imagine a couple who routinely thank each other or express appreciation at the end of the day. They share brief instances in which they feel supported, loved or valued while encouraging a practice of gratitude and recognition. In addition to strengthening their relationship, this practice helps them focus on positive aspects and reaffirms their commitment to one another when faced with adversity.

Couples must be prepared to make active investments in their relationship if they want to feel the depth and richness of covenant love. This entails making time for each other a priority and putting aside outside distractions so they can concentrate on strengthening their bond. It involves being in the moment, paying close attention, and reacting with compassion and understanding. As partners cultivate these behaviors, they build a marriage that exemplifies the kind, patient, and enduring love described in scripture as divine.

Couples who cultivate covenant love leave a legacy of dedication and commitment that impacts generations. Their union turns into a monument to the strength of unwavering devotion and love. For those who want to understand the profound beauty of a relationship founded on divine principles, it serves as a source of inspiration and guidance.

Unwavering dedication, devoted love, and grace are the foundations of God's covenant with His people (Isaiah 54:10). In marriage, couples should strive for this kind of unconditional, selfless love. Forgiveness and grace are fundamental components of covenant love. As God has forgiven us, spouses in a marriage must also be quick to forgive (Ephesians 4:32).

This grace-based forgiveness promotes healing, reconciliation, and keeps the marriage strong even in the face of adversity.

Reflection: Think about how these ideas can change your marriage into one that is characterized by grace and resiliency as you reflect on the function of covenant love. Seize the chance to strengthen your bond with your spouse and build a relationship that not only endures but thrives in the face of aging. May this insight make your marriage a lighthouse of love and hope for everyone who sees it.

Chapter 2

Building a Christ-Centered Marriage

Praying Together Strengthens Spiritual Bonds

Prayer is two-way communication with our Heavenly Father. It should be a divine act of unity in a Christ-centered marriage, not a spiritual exercise engaged in for tradition's sake. Jesus frequently withdrew to pray, establishing sacred moments for spiritual communion (Luke 5:16). By joining together in prayer, a husband and wife mirror Jesus' action and welcome God into their daily lives. Prayer strengthens a couple's emotional and spiritual bond while binding their hearts and allowing them to be open to God's guidance and wisdom. Praying together is a profound practice that strengthens the spiritual intimacy of marriage and goes beyond simple devotion. Harmony and understanding are established by opening up to the Heart of God and one another simultaneously. Through inviting heavenly guidance into the marital relationship a sacred space is created, strengthening the marriage with love and intention.

A daily devotional practice provides a structured approach to connecting with God and one another. Hearts are aligned in accordance with God's will as prayer and gratitude is verbalized. Jesus taught us to knock, seek, and ask in Matthew 7:7. Couples pray to God for wisdom, blessings, and fortitude. When combined, prayer turns everyday activities into heavenly opportunities to deepen relationship with Christ and each other. Whether through predawn prayer time, prayer walks in nature, or prayer journaling in the quiet corners of home, these practices encourage reflection, gratitude and grace. Praying together aloud enables both hearts to unite as one and for requests to be granted, as stated in Matthew 18:19: "If two of you agree here on earth concerning anything you ask, my Father in heaven will do it for you."(NLT)

Commitment and intentionality are necessities to establish a regular prayer routine. Uniting in prayer in the morning or evening provides time for spiritual connection and helps to frame the day with purpose and serenity. By inviting God to be a part of daily life and important decisions, dependence on His wisdom is strengthened. To make sure this habit becomes a vital part of marriage, choose times that work for both parties. Consistency is the key. When there is consistency in meeting God at a particular time and place, He is faithful to show up and His Presence continually grows stronger in that space.

Different types of prayer address different marital needs. Through divine intervention, you can express care and support by lifting each other's burdens to God through intercessory prayers. A spirit of appreciation is fostered by prayers of thanksgiving and gratitude, which change the focus from difficulties to blessings (Moore, 2023). By emphasizing positive traits and contributions spouses bring, the lens through which they are seen changes.

Praying together allows you to witness God's power in your marriage. Be prepared. Uniting in prayer will not occur without attempts to thwart the decision. The goal of Satan is to keep you divided because he knows the power the two of you possess when you are united. PRESS THROUGH!!!

Barriers may arise due to differences in comfort levels or prayer styles, but they can be overcome with patience and honest communication. Finding common ground and discussing preferences lays the foundation for inclusive practices that respect the spiritual expressions of both spouses. Distractions must be put aside to create a focused, interruption-free environment where quality time with God and one another is spent. This may require turning off phones or finding a peaceful area to connect without distractions.

According to Matthew 18:20, the Bible says that He is present among His people when two or more are gathered in His name. Couples who gather to pray together experience the strength of Christ's presence which deepens their relationship and helps them navigate through difficult times. Praying together serves as a reminder that you are never alone in your struggles, particularly during life's darkest moments. God is ever-present and provides consolation and serenity (Philippians 4:6-7).

The deeper your prayer time becomes, the more you transition into worship which ushers you into a different place where the supernatural power of breakthrough occurs. When a husband and wife worship together and surrender to God, they enter a realm beyond time where healing occurs, transformation takes place, and breakthrough is evident. You enter an audience before the King, who honors covenant.

Consider setting aside time every week to reflect on your shared prayers and acknowledge those that have been answered with thanksgiving, continuously surrender those that have not. Talk about the effects these experiences have had on your relationship and spiritual development. Make a note of any modifications or responses you receive, and express gratitude for the journey you are on together. In addition to strengthening your relationship, this activity provides a deeper understanding of how God is at work in your marriage.

When attempting to create a marriage centered on Christ, remember that prayer is a lifestyle not just an activity. It is an ongoing dialogue with God, relying on His grace and wisdom to strengthen your relationship.

Embracing Grace and Patience

A marriage centered on Christian principles requires grace and patience. Paul exhorts believers in Ephesians 4:32 to be kind and compassionate toward one another, forgiving one another as God did for them in Christ. When marriage is viewed through the lens of grace, it becomes a reflection of Christ's love for the Church. Just as Christ extends grace to mankind despite our faults, so too should spouses extend grace to one another. This grace enables you to look past one another's flaws and to cherish the person behind the imperfections, thus forgiving one another with empathy and understanding. A supportive environment, where being vulnerable is safe and growth is possible, is created by reacting to your spouse's mistakes with grace rather than criticism.

According to Galatians 5:22–23, patience is a fruit of the Spirit and is essential to preserving a marriage centered on Christ. According to 1 Corinthians 13:4, the Bible reminds us that love is patient and kind. Patience, a quality that is often tested in daily life, facilitates resilience and development. It enables spouses to support one another while tackling challenges together. Patience allows both spouses' viewpoints to be shared during disagreements, promoting understanding rather than hostility. During trying times when answers appear to be distant, waiting is where patience becomes an act of faith. A stronger marriage bond and a greater sense of unity are fostered by waiting with hope and faith on God's timing. Patience keeps the relationship peaceful by promoting the belief that love will win out and that a solution will be found. In these situations, exercising patience involves being present in the moment, paying attention, and resisting the urge to act impulsively.

It is impossible to overestimate the importance of patience and grace in marriage. These qualities help spouses feel secure and appreciated. Feelings of emotional safety increase as trust is fostered through regular displays of kindness and grace. When both spouses make a commitment to respecting these values, a healthy relationship is developed, fostering an atmosphere where everyone is inspired to grow and flourish. When patience and grace are prioritized, mutual support comes naturally.

Reflecting Christ's Love in Everyday Actions

Each interaction within a marriage offers an opportunity to demonstrate Christ's love, transforming everyday encounters into meaningful acts of devotion. Demonstrating this commitment is best achieved through tangible acts of kindness and service that extend beyond verbal expression. Consider completing a chore your spouse dislikes or simply making coffee in the manner desired. Despite the size of these gestures, they convey consideration and care. A gentle reminder of love and appreciation, echoing the selfless love of Christ to your spouse.

In any relationship, words have great power. Your spouse can feel more confident and valuable if you speak encouraging and affirming words. Imagine the joy that fills the heart when compliments are expressed of identified abilities or gratefulness shared for being a part of life's journey. Affirmation creates a foundation of gratitude and trust, fostering an atmosphere where love can thrive. Positive utterances are seeds sown into the soil of your marriage that blossom into a beautiful garden of mutual respect and appreciation.

Christ's love for the Church is reflected in sacrificial love, which embodies a dedication that goes beyond selfish interests. It requires you to show your spouse your undying love and support. Sacrificial love is about making daily choices to put your spouse's welfare first, not about extravagant displays of affection. According to John 13:34, Jesus urged His disciples to love one another as He loved them. It demonstrates the vastness of your love, whether it is by offering support through trying times or paying close attention when personal talk time is needed. A willingness to fully give of oneself without anticipating anything in return is reflected in this type of love. This love is reciprocal. When exercised by both parties, marriage remains healthy and efficient. In reflecting this love, healing of past hurts can occur, promoting understanding and forgiveness. It fosters a loving atmosphere where both spouses are comfortable sharing their weaknesses and anxieties. Because of the open communication this environment fosters, both spouses can approach problems with empathy and compassion. Based on unfailing love, rebuilding trust strengthens the bond between the two parties.

Creating a Legacy of Faith and Love

Consider the legacy you want to leave behind - one that encompasses love, faith and financial prosperity. Leaving a legacy based on your faith entails passing down customs that align with your values and beliefs. It is more than just teaching; it is about modeling a Christ-centered lifestyle for children. Parents are instructed in Deuteronomy 6:6-7 to instill God's commands in their children and to discuss with them throughout the day His statues. You can ingrain values that will guide them throughout their lives by demonstrating faith in your daily actions. Long after you are gone, this legacy serves as a beacon to guide their path. Focus on incorporating faith into your family's everyday life, to ensure it remains a cornerstone of your life.

Building a legacy of faith and love is more than passing on religious tradition; it is about creating a living testament to the values that define your family. Family devotionals and Bible studies provide opportunities to discuss spiritual lessons with one another. When significant days are observed with intention, they are transformed from simple customs into manifestations of faith. Reinforcing these celebrations by sharing history to emphasize purpose supports these customs and allows faith to permeate every aspect of family life.

Future generations and your immediate family will benefit from having a solid spiritual foundation. Others can be inspired and encouraged to grow when personal testimonies and spiritual journeys are shared. You offer timeless wisdom by sharing stories of people who have overcome adversity through faith. Examples of faith in action provide strength and applicability. Your descendants will have the means to delve deeply into their beliefs if you promote spiritual education. In the face of life's uncertainties, this foundation serves as an anchor providing stability and direction. The influence of your faith endures beyond your lifetime as each generation builds upon this heritage.

It takes both introspection and action to honor and preserve this legacy. Creating a scrapbook or family faith journal helps capture memories for future generations by safeguarding moments of spiritual significance. These gatherings promote a sense of belonging by highlighting shared values and experiences. Participating in family gatherings throughout the year incorporates faith, reinforces connections, and provides occasions to recognize achievements and reaffirm commitments. Such events may include meaningful discussions, worship, or shared meals, all of which contribute to a spirit of unity and collaboration within the family. By actively nurturing this legacy, you ensure its vitality for years to come.

Legacy Scrapbook Activity

With your family, think about creating a "Legacy Scrapbook." Record significant anniversaries, group prayers, and thoughts on how your faith has impacted your lives. Invite everyone in the family to share their memories and ideas. Through shared storytelling, this collaborative project not only protects your legacy but also strengthens family bonds.

Building a legacy of faith and love is about more than passing on stories and traditions; it is about creating a living testament to the values that define your family. While adding to a shared story of love and devotion, this legacy encourages each member to develop spiritually. By recording personal accounts or documenting collective experiences, you create a record of family faith history intended to inform future generations. Maintaining this mindset helps establish a basis for faith to continue as an influence in the future.

A Christ-centered marriage is a journey of continuous growth and reflection. By integrating prayer, worship, grace, and love into your marriage, you build a legacy and create a union that reflects divine love and purpose.

Chapter 3

Men & Women - God's Design
Appreciating the Differences Between the Two

Men and women are God's amazing creation. Understanding the differences between the two is essential for building the cornerstones of marriage, effective communication, healthy relationships and deeper intimacy. These differences impact various aspects of life, from how we think and process emotions to how we approach spirituality and experience physical intimacy. When we understand and appreciate these distinctions, we can better respect and collaborate with one another.

Mental Differences: Cognitive Strengths

Men and women commonly show distinct cognitive strengths. Men often perform better in spatial tasks, object manipulation, navigation, and logi- cal categorization.

Women often excel at verbal communication, multitasking, and social understanding such as reading emotions and interpreting social cues. Women are often better at empathizing, identifying, and responding appropriately to others' emotions and perspectives.

As Proverbs 2:6 reminds us, "For the Lord gives wisdom; from his mouth come knowledge and understanding."(NIV) God is the source of all wisdom, and He encourages the cultivation of cognitive abilities in both men and women. Each person's unique cognitive strengths are gifts to be developed and used for good. These differences result from a combination of biological factors such as brain structure and hormonal influences, as well as environmental and cultural factors that shape how these abilities are developed and expressed.

Patterns of Emotional Processing

The way men and women process emotions often follows different patterns. Men tend to process feelings in a more compartmentalized manner and may avoid dealing with emotions until resolution is available. This is not an emotional deficiency (as women often believe); it is simply a different way of doing things. Men may struggle with expressing vulnerability, often seeking to fix problems rather than discussing their feelings in depth.

Women tend to process emotions more holistically, discussing and reflecting on them frequently to understand and regulate their emotional experiences. They are more likely to seek emotional validation and want to talk through their feelings as part of the processing experience. However, when discussing their feelings, wives are often not seeking their husbands to provide a solution to fix the situation, but rather a listening ear to release it from their hearts and minds.

Women are inclined to store conversations more readily by emotionally processing for later detailed recall. Unfortunately, men often forget the conversation or fail to recognize its implications until it is replayed weeks, months, or years later, because of the way they process it.

It is important to note that all individuals do not fit this general pattern of processing emotions. Personality, culture, life experiences, and individual temperament all influence how one handles emotions. Neither approach is better than the other; each is simply a different lens through which life is viewed.

Problem-Solving and Decision Making

Men are inclined to approach problems with a linear, logical, and solution-focused mindset. They often prefer to solve problems independently and may feel frustrated if issues are not resolved quickly.

Women tend to consider different perspectives and emotional aspects of a situation when making decisions. They may value collaborative discussions that include various viewpoints and potential impacts on the relationship.

Proverbs 3:5-6 encourages both approaches while pointing to ultimate wisdom: "Trust in the Lord with all your heart and lean not on your own understanding; in all your ways submit to him, and he will make your paths straight."(NIV) This reminds us to rely on God's guidance in decision-making, whether we approach problems linearly or collaboratively.

When both approaches are valued and utilized, communication in the relationship is significantly improved. The linear approach can lead to efficient solutions, while the collaborative approach can ensure that all perspectives are considered and both partners feel heard.

Physical Differences

The physical appearance of men and women are the most obvious differences. Men generally have a larger frame, higher muscle mass, and greater bone density. Testosterone drives characteristics like facial hair, deeper voices, faster metabolism rates, and a greater inclination to develop muscle mass.

Women generally have a higher percentage of body fat, which supports reproductive functions and overall health. Estrogen affects characteristics such as broader hips, larger breasts, and the physiological systems related to childbearing, including the uterus, menstrual cycle, and the ability to breastfeed.

God created man and woman differently with distinct roles and purposes. These differences develop and change across life stages, with hormonal influences varying significantly during puberty, reproductive years, and aging. Understanding this helps us appreciate how physical needs and capabilities can shift throughout life and how to best support one another during these changes.

Power of Hormonal Influences

Hormones play a significant role in affecting everything from energy levels to emotional responses and physical capabilities.

Men have higher levels of testosterone, which influences not only physical characteristics but also aggression, competitive behaviors, sex drive, muscle growth, and fat distribution patterns.

Women experience the complexity of estrogen and progesterone, which influence mood, energy levels, fertility, and emotional regulation. The menstrual cycle creates a regular change in energy, cravings, emotions, and physical comfort.

1Peter 3:7 acknowledges these realities: "Husbands, in the same way be considerate as you live with your wives, and treat them with respect as the weaker partner and as heirs with you of the gracious gift of life."(NIV) This verse acknowledges physical differences between men and women, including hormonal influences, while emphasizing the importance of mutual respect in marriage.

Physical Strength and Endurance

Men are generally stronger in terms of raw physical strength due to higher muscle mass and testosterone levels. They tend to excel in activities that require explosive strength and power, often performing better in sports or tasks that demand short bursts of intense physical effort.

Women tend to have greater flexibility, balance, and endurance in tasks or activities that last longer. They often recover faster from certain types of injuries and may have better pain tolerance and different muscle recovery that serve them well in childbirth and endurance activities.

While these are general trends, it is essential to remember that some women are physically stronger than some men, and individual training, genetics, and personal dedication play significant roles.

Emotional Expression

Men and women often express emotions differently, mainly due to a combination of biological tendencies and cultural conditioning. Men are typically less expressive of their feelings and are often conditioned from an early age to hide their vulnerability. This does not mean they feel less deeply or hurt less; they may express emotions differently or in more private settings.

Women are generally more openly expressive and verbal about emotions. They may be more comfortable sharing feelings and may process emotions through talking and sharing with others.

Much of this difference stems from cultural conditioning rather than biological necessity. Understanding these patterns can help individuals communicate more effectively while avoiding harmful stereotypes about how men or women "should" express emotions.

Emotional Regulation

When men encounter emotional distress, they generally focus on problem-solving. They often want to identify the issue, develop a solution, and implement it quickly. For practical problems, this approach can be very effective. However, this is not always the best approach when dealing with concerns of the heart as they relate to sensitive issues within the relationship that are not a quick fix but require time and attention.

Women are more likely to focus on the emotional experience itself and seek emotional validation. They may want to discuss their feelings, understand the emotional impact, and feel heard and supported before moving on to solutions. Appreciating the balance that men bring to developing a solution can often help guide a couple toward a resolution, preventing them from becoming stuck in a situation that can be resolved with effort and commitment.

Understanding these tendencies can help couples communicate more effectively by recognizing when problem-solving is needed versus when emotional support is required. Sometimes the most loving response is to listen and validate rather than offering solutions.

Social and Environmental Influences

Cultural conditioning often discourages men from expressing vulnerability, sometimes leading to emotional suppression that can be harmful to their minds and bodies over time. Men benefit from safe spaces to express and process emotions. Although they often do not express it, it comes out in other ways such as isolation and aggression. Consequently, men need to have positive male relationships where they feel secure enough to express themselves. Men build relationships with other men around things they do (basketball, video-gaming, car club, golf).

Women are socially encouraged to express and articulate emotions, which can be healthy, but sometimes leads to over-processing or excessive emotional focus that interferes with problem-solving. Healthy female friendships are important as they provide a space to share, grow, and build confidence in a way that differs from the wife's relationship with her spouse.

Romans 12:15 provides balance: "Rejoice with those who rejoice; mourn with those who mourn."(NIV) This highlights the importance of sharing emotional states with one another, regardless of gender.

Proverbs 4:23 encourage careful emotional management: "Above all else, guard your heart, for everything you do flows from it."(NIV) The author King Solomon encourages thoughtful management of emotions in all relationship dynamics.

These patterns should not be used to dismiss or minimize your spouse's emotional experiences or needs, but rather to better understand when the need arises.

Sexual Health

Men are generally less likely to experience sexual dysfunction related to emotional factors and may be more influenced by physical health issues, stress, or fatigue.

Women find that emotional and relational issues like stress, relationship dissatisfaction, or feeling disconnected can significantly impact sexual desire and function. Their sexual health is often more holistically connected to overall well-being.

Sexual health encompasses physical, emotional, and relational aspects for both spouses. Creating an environment of emotional safety, physical health, and relational connection benefits everyone.

Biological Basis of Sexual Desire

Men generally experience more spontaneous desire and are more visual in their sexual arousal. Their desire may be triggered more easily by physical or visual stimuli and may feel more urgent or immediate with less psychological involvement.

Women often experience sexual desire that is more emotional and contextual, not solely dependent on physical stimuli. Emotional intimacy, mental connection, and psychological factors such as mood, stress levels, and feelings of security are significant factors in female arousal. Therefore, her sexual desire is tied to relationship dynamics, trust, and emotional closeness.

In the minds of women, intimacy and sex are not the same. Intimacy is activities such as cuddling, holding hands, caressing, talking, laughing, playing together, and do not necessarily have to end with sexual intercourse.

Sexual desire patterns vary significantly among individuals and can change across life stages and circumstances. What matters most is understanding and respecting your spouse's unique patterns and needs.

Sexual Arousal and Satisfaction

Men generally have more obvious physical responses to sexual stimuli and may reach arousal more quickly. Their sexual response may be more straightforward and physically focused.

Women's sexual satisfaction is often more psychological and relational. They may require more time, emotional safety, and connection to reach sexual fulfillment. The emotional context usually plays a larger role in their sexual experience.

Both partners benefit from understanding these general patterns while recognizing their spouse's unique needs, design, and preferences. Communication, connection, and patience are essential for mutual satisfaction and intimacy, and will be discussed in later chapters.

Erogenous Zones

Both men and women have numerous erogenous zones in the body that are extremely sensitive to stimulation and were designed by an omniscient (all-knowing) God for arousal and pleasure. Listed below are only a few.

Men's erogenous zones include but are not limited to the genitals (penis and scrotum), which are hypersensitive to touch and stimulation; the nipples, neck, and surprisingly, the soles of his feet are also areas of arousal.

Women's erogenous zones include but are not limited to the genital area (clitoris, vulva, and vagina), breast, neck, inner thighs, and lower back. The clitoris has thousands of nerve endings that when stimulated, create intense pleasure. These areas are highly sensitive to touch and play a significant role in sexual arousal.

Differences in How Desire Is Experienced

Men often experience more immediate and physical desire for sex. Their arousal may be more direct and can be triggered by visual or physical stimuli relatively quickly. Most men do not have to be emotionally connected to desire sexual engagement. When the relationship is in distress, to the woman's dismay, the man will often still desire sexual relations.

Women's sexual desire is often strongly influenced by emotional closeness and relational dynamics. They usually feel desire within the context of emotional connection and relational intimacy, and may need to feel emotionally safe and connected before sexual desire emerges. Therefore, when there is a disconnect in the relationship, it is not unusual for the wife to experience little to no arousal and to be uninterested in sexual engagement.

Understanding these patterns can help couples develop better intimacy by addressing both physical and emotional needs in the relationship.

Desire and Communication

Men's desire may be more direct and physical, which can sometimes lead to miscommunication if emotional needs are not acknowledged or addressed first.

The emotional state of the relationship can significantly influence a woman's desire. Verbal and non-verbal expressions of love, appreciation, and connection are often highly significant in developing her context for desire.

Proverbs 5:18-19 encourages mutual affection: "May your fountain be blessed, and may you rejoice in the wife of your youth... may her breasts satisfy you always, may you be ever captivated by her love."(NIV) This passage encourages mutual affection and desire in marriage, highlighting the importance of ongoing connection and appreciation.

Many women desire and enjoy sex as much as men do (some even more). However, due to societal and cultural beliefs, it is often frowned upon, encouraging women to suppress their sexual desire and pleasure. Therefore, feeling safe to be vulnerable is crucial for open and honest communication about desires and needs to occur. This will strengthen intimacy and prevent misunderstandings. Both spouses need to feel heard, valued, and desired.

Factors Influencing Desire in Relationships

For many men, physical appearance, sexual attraction, and novelties are influential in sparking and maintaining desire. Visual connection and physical affection often play crucial roles in their relationship.

For most women, relationship satisfaction, emotional connection, and security play a significant role in igniting desire. Feeling valued, appreciated, and emotionally connected often creates the foundation for sexual desire.

1 Corinthians 13:4-7 describes foundational love: "Love is patient, love is kind... It always protects, always trusts, always hopes, always perseveres."(NIV) This highlights the importance of love as a foundation for deep emotional and sexual intimacy.

Sacrificial love, grounded in mutual respect and care, enhances desire and intimacy over the long term. Ephesians 5:25 calls for sacrificial love: "Husbands, love your wives, just as Christ loved the Church and gave himself up for her."(NIV)

Healthy relationships encompass both physical attraction and emotional connection, for fostering sustained intimacy throughout marriage.

Understanding the differences between men and women across mental, physical, emotional, sexual, and relational dimensions can significantly enrich your marital relationship. When these differences are approached through both scientific understanding and biblical wisdom, tools are accessed for deeper communication, intimacy, and connection.

These differences are not obstacles to overcome but gifts to appreciate and utilize. They reflect God's design for complementarity, where two different people come together to create something beautiful and complete that neither could achieve alone.

Every person is unique, created in God's image with his/her own combination of traits, gifts, and characteristics. While understanding general patterns can be helpful, getting to know your spouse as an individual is far more important than any general principle. Growing in understanding of oneself and one's spouse teaches how to love more effectively and serve each other better.

This information should never be used to justify discrimination, limit opportunities, or dismiss individual experiences and capabilities. The goal is to enhance love and respect in your relationship by providing knowledge and greater appreciation for the commonalities and differences between you. Using these insights to foster understanding and cooperation, without stereotyping, limiting, or dismissing your spouse, will help prevent various situations from arising. Remember, familial history, life experiences, and cultural influences all affect the person you and your spouse have become.

When we understand and honor the ways God has made us different, we can work together more effectively, love each other more completely, and build marriages that reflect His design for human relationships. These differences, properly understood and applied, become tools for building a stronger, more intimate, and more satisfying marriage that honors both spouses and glorifies God.

Chapter 4

Communication as the Cornerstone

MASTERING THE ART OF Actively Listening to Your Spouse

In the quiet of an evening meal, a couple sits facing one another, and the silence between them is louder than their words. Although they are aware of one another's presence, neither of them is paying much attention to the other. This scene is familiar in many homes, where the daily grind and societal distractions frequently overpower true communication and the art of listening and being emotionally present. Active listening is not only about hearing words; it is about listening intentionally to gain understanding of your spouse's perspective. This ideology reflects the biblical principle of being "quick to listen, slow to speak" (James 1:19 NIV). Intentional listening encourages deep conversations that go beyond simple interactions. It strengthens the basis of your relationship by allowing empathy and understanding.

It takes deliberate effort to engage in the practice of active listening. You must listen not to respond but to understand. The Bible exhorts us to live in harmony and to bear each other's burdens (Galatians 6:2, Romans 12:16). One way to bear your spouse's emotional burden and demonstrate mutual care in a marriage is to listen actively. Deepening understanding can be achieved by using strategies like mirroring, which involves repeating back to your spouse what has been said. Spouses feel reassured that emotions are being acknowledged when words are paraphrased reflecting their thoughts and feelings. Allowing your spouse to express himself/herself fully without interruption demonstrates respect and creates an atmosphere where genuine understanding can flourish. Proverbs 18:13 reminds us that it is foolish and shameful to respond before listening. Interruptions can cause frustration or resentment and act as barriers to understanding. By avoiding interruptions, you allow your spouse the opportunity to express their concerns and ideas without feeling ignored. Uninterrupted attentiveness transforms routine conversations into opportunities for growth and understanding, creating a relationship built on love and respect.

Pausing after your spouse has finished speaking is another effective tactic. Moments of silence, while seemingly minor, can offer the space needed for thoughtful reflection. Waiting before answering is similar to the biblical advice to "be still and know that I am God" (Psalm 46:10 NIV). We are often better able to understand the heart behind the words, as well as the words themselves, when we are silent.

It is crucial to establish an environment that fosters open and candid communication. Couples should look for times and locations for peaceful, undisturbed conversation, just as Jesus retreated to quiet areas to pray (Luke 5:16). Removing distractions like phones and other electronics promotes a closer bond by allowing both partners to prioritize each other.

Two essential components of active listening are presence and patience. The Bible teaches that love is patient (1 Corinthians 13:4). Being patient allows your spouse to express thoughts and emotions without feeling disregarded. It creates a space for emotional development and connection, allowing you to hear the feelings that lie beneath the words. You can listen without assumptions when you practice mindfulness, which is being present in every moment. According to Proverbs 19:11, "A person's wisdom yields patience; it is to one's glory to overlook an offense."(NIV) When we listen patiently, we allow our hearts to see beyond the present moment and embrace the bigger picture. It is essential to acknowledge and put aside one's own prejudices. These prejudices influence how you interpret what your spouse says, often leading to miscommunication or conflict. By setting aside personal opinions, you allow yourself to see things from your spouse's point of view, which promotes empathy and connection.

It takes more than just nodding in agreement to establish trust when you listen to your spouse; it also entails validating feelings and comprehending what is being conveyed. According to Proverbs 15:1, "A gentle answer turns away wrath, but a harsh word stirs up anger."(NIV) By practicing active listening, a safe space is created where both spouses can freely express their feelings and develop deeper intimacy. Continuously practicing active listening builds intimacy and trust, enabling both spouses to express themselves freely without inhibition. Following up on earlier discussions shows attentiveness and willingness to work through problems and share successes.

Strengthening Bonds

Consider a recent discussion where the results could have been different with active listening. If you had listened intently and patiently, how might your response have changed? Consider using strategies such as waiting for pauses before speaking or mirroring your spouse's words. Write down the things you recognize about your engagement and the changes you want to make in future discussions to improve your relationship.

Nonverbal Communication in Marriage

When words fail, your body speaks volumes. One effective strategy for improving communication in marriage is to recognize and interpret body language. Unspoken cues often reveal more profound truths. Jesus frequently expressed love and understanding through his actions and body language (Mark 1:41, Matthew 9:36). Understanding nonverbal clues can help to gain a better understanding of your spouse's inner world. Actual feelings and thoughts can be inferred from partners' gestures and facial expressions. A gentle smile or a furrowing of the brow can express approval or discomfort, respectively. Being aware of these cues enables you to react with wisdom and compassion. Crossed arms may be interpreted as defensiveness, while an open posture is often linked to receptiveness. These behaviors are commonly correlated with the particular thought patterns, but they are not definite indicators. By paying attention to these nonverbal clues, you can have more compassionate and clear conversations.

Another powerful nonverbal communication method that expresses love and support is touch. A gentle hug or a soft pat on the shoulder can convey support and empathy. When discussing delicate subjects, holding hands can create a feeling of safety and unity. Touch strengthens the emotional connection between spouses by acting as a bridge to reinforce the bond between them. According to 1Corinthians 13:13, "And now these three remain: faith, hope, and love. But, love is the greatest of these."(NIV) Touch is one of the most powerful expressions of love, transcending words. Physical distance, however, can signal emotional disconnect. When spouses drift apart physically, it often reflects underlying tensions or unresolved issues. Emotional bonds can be preserved and strengthened by being aware of the part touch plays in your relationship.

Tone and inflection in your voice can change the meaning of what you say and affect how your spouse interprets it. While an accusatory tone may increase tension, a gentle tone can soften criticism and make it more acceptable. According to Proverbs 15:4, "The soothing tongue is a tree of life, but a perverse tongue crushes the spirit."(NIV) Practicing modulation helps prevent miscommunication and guarantees that your message is understood. To promote openness and trust during delicate conversations, emphasize a positive tone. Even the most severe criticism can be turned into a productive discussion depending on the tone you use. With this strategy, your spouse is encouraged to participate without feeling threatened or defensive. Reconciliation can be facilitated and tensions reduced with a soothing, compassionate tone.

Making eye contact and using visual cues are essential in demonstrating respect and attention during discussions. Maintaining eye contact with your spouse conveys interest and involvement in the conversation. It shows that you are paying attention to the conversation and are present. Communication attempts can be hindered by avoiding eye contact or using negative visual cues such as eye-rolling, which can convey disrespect or disinterest. These subtle visual cues significantly impact your spouse's perception of your engagement and sincerity in the conversation. Therefore, being aware of these cues can improve communication and understanding.

The power of non-verbal communication in marital relationships should not be underestimated. It enhances verbal communication by giving more depth to exchanges. By engaging positively through these silent signals, you strengthen your interaction. Every touch, look, and gesture adds levels of meaning that words cannot express.

Consider a couple that frequently quarrels over misunderstandings. During their conversations, they consciously decide to pay close attention to each other's nonverbal cues, including posture, tone, and gestures. They eventually discover that these nonverbal clues enable them to resolve problems before they escalate. Through awareness of the atmosphere in the room, couples reduce the need to apologize or rebuild weeks, months, and years of progress that is torn down in a moment of disagreement. Their conversations are calmer and clearer as a result of this new understanding which lessens conflict and increases intimacy. Couples become closer by learning to comprehend one another in ways that go beyond words, while reflecting the biblical idea that "two are better than one" (Ecclesiastes 4:9 NIV).

It takes patience and practice to integrate an awareness of nonverbal communication into your marriage. Additionally, nonverbal communication creates a supportive and empathetic atmosphere. You can show that you understand and respect your spouse's needs and feelings by responding to silent cues. This attentiveness strengthens the emotional bond between you and builds trust. Awareness of the silent cues eventually become instinctive, resulting in a smooth communication flow that strengthens marriage and enhances the relationship.

Relationships are enhanced when both verbal and nonverbal communication are mastered. You can learn about your spouse's needs and feelings by paying attention to tone, body language, and other nonverbal cues. As with all relationships, communication is the cornerstone of unity, love, and trust; values that have their roots in biblical teachings. By investing in these qualities, you cultivate a marriage founded on love, respect, and understanding.

Empathy Driven Dialogue

Biblical teachings on love, understanding, and humility aligns with the role empathy plays in communication. It forms the foundation for meaningful conversation by influencing how you perceive and relate to your spouse. The adage of 'walking in your *spouse's* shoes' is directly related to the Bible's exhortation to "bear one another's burdens" (Galatians 6:2 NIV). Think back to a time when your significant other complained about having a hectic schedule. Take a moment to acknowledge the feelings expressed rather than answering with a list of your own stressors. By recognizing and ministering to the needs of your spouse, as Jesus did during His ministry to those around Him, you are reflecting Christ's love. (Philippians 2:4-5). We are called to listen intently and validate the feelings of people we care about, just as He did when He heard the anguish of those around Him and offered consolation and compassion.

When practicing empathy, it is vital to keep in mind the following principle from James 1:19: "Everyone should be quick to listen, slow to speak, and slow to become angry."(NIV) This practice encourages one to take a pause similar to the one mentioned when your spouse expresses frustration, allowing emotions to be heard and understood before responding. Jesus Himself often responded with compassion, as seen in His response to the woman caught in adultery when He offered forgiveness rather than condemnation (John 8:10-11). This model of empathy sets the foundation for a marriage where both partners feel respected and loved.

One effective way to communicate emotions without placing blame is by using "I" statements. The significance of speaking the truth in love is emphasized in the Bible (Ephesians 4:15). Just as Christ invited His followers into the tranquility of His presence saying, "I feel unheard," it invites your spouse into a place of vulnerability and strengthens your emotional bond. It creates a safer atmosphere for conversation by focusing on your feelings rather than making accusations against your spouse. "I" statements allow you to express your needs and emotions clearly and concisely, facilitating open communication. They invite your spouse into your emotional realm without making him/her accountable for your feelings.

Empathic listening significantly improves emotional bonds. In addition to demonstrating that you are there for your spouse during life's emotional journeys, this type of listening reaffirms commitment to be supportive in all stages of life. Be mindful of the emotions that are not expressed during conversations. Sometimes, deeper emotions remain unspoken because words only scratch the surface. It takes sensitivity and connection to recognize these feelings, but doing so improves your relationship.

The Bible instructs us to react to disagreements with kindness and grace rather than harshness. Empathy in times of conflict is a reflection of God's patience and love for us. When both spouses approach disagreements with kindness and humility, they create an atmosphere that is conducive to healing and growth.

Your relationship's foundation is strengthened when you integrate empathy into your daily interactions which promote love and unity. Love is kind, patient, and not easily agitated, as stated in 1 Corinthians 13:4–7. These qualities form the foundation of empathetic communication, in which both parties make an effort to understand one another and develop a bond characterized by respect and concern for each other. Take a moment to calm down and respond with kindness rather than rage or blame. Saying something like, "I understand this is frustrating for both of us," helps to reduce tension and demonstrates your willingness to work towards a solution. Your relationship is further strengthened when you offer assistance during difficult times. Saying, "I'm here for you" can be a very comforting gesture. By placing empathy at the center of your marriage, you allow Christ's transforming love to shape your bond and bring about deeper intimacy, understanding, and healing. Compassionate responses in disagreements can transform conflict into an opportunity for growth. When tensions arise, practice non-defensive responses. Empathy-driven dialogue does not require that you agree on everything, but that space is created where both voices are valued. During disagreements, it is necessary to listen intently and react thoughtfully for trust and intimacy to grow. To establish a foundation of love and respect, it is important to acknowledge each other's feelings and respond with compassion.

In conversations, empathy can be rewarding and challenging. It requires setting aside personal biases to fully engage with each other's experiences. This engagement is about being present in the moment, free from preconceived ideas and distractions.

Consider implementing mindfulness exercises into your daily routine to improve empathy-driven communication in your marriage. By practicing presence and awareness, mindfulness enables you to interact more thoroughly with your spouse's feelings and thoughts. Before having difficult conversations, you can help yourself by practicing basic techniques such as deep breathing, prayer or meditation.

Frequent check-ins with one another also foster empathy-driven conversation. These times offer opportunities to discuss emotions or worries before they become more serious problems. You demonstrate a commitment to actively nurturing your relationship by maintaining open lines of communication.

Incorporating empathy into your daily interactions transforms how you communicate with your spouse. Conversations change from surface-level interactions into dialogues that are meaningful. Spouses have profound appreciation and understanding for one another when they engage regularly in empathy-driven conversation.

As you continue to explore empathy in your marriage, remember that it is an ongoing process requiring patience and dedication. The benefits are profound, creating a deeper connection founded on compassion, trust, and mutual respect.

By fostering an environment where empathy thrives, you create a marriage that reflects the beauty of two individuals coming together as one while honoring each other's unique perspectives and experiences.

Overcoming Communication Breakdowns

Unaddressed communication breakdowns can affect relationships. The initial step in resolving issues is to identify the underlying causes of breakdowns. Communication may be impacted by stressful life events, such as job loss or health problems, which can leave spouses less responsive to each other's needs. Misinterpretations and assumptions can also hinder mutual understanding and create distance in relationships. These often arise from relating past experiences to current situations resulting in misplaced reactions. Early recognition of these factors can help prevent escalation.

Improving communication involves practical approaches that encourage clarity and patience. Being able to recognize when a conversation is not being productive is important. For example, taking breaks during arguments allows both parties time to reflect and calm down. However, it is necessary to revisit the discussion at an agreed upon time to address the issue, as it will resurface if left unresolved.

Establishing rules of engagement during times of peace is beneficial. A more productive conversation can be achieved by establishing guidelines like taking turns speaking or managing conversational turns with a talking token or stick. By reducing stress and encouraging a more positive dialogue, these techniques enable couples to resolve their disagreements more effectively.

After a breakdown, it is critical to reestablish open lines of communication as promptly as possible. Frequent check-ins become vital instruments for resolving outstanding issues and preventing them from escalating. These discussions should be planned so that a specific time is allotted for discussing issues without interruptions. This process can be facilitated, if necessary, by using communication tools such as journals or apps. These tools make it easier to communicate complicated emotions by providing ways of expressing ideas and feelings. Another strategy for reestablishing effective communication is participating in teamwork, such as playing team sports or cooking together. These tools serve as links between spouses promoting an atmosphere conducive to open and honest communication, that ultimately strengthens the relationship.

The role of apology and reconciliation cannot be overstated in mending relationship rifts. Saying "I'm sorry" is not enough to constitute a sincere apology; it requires acknowledging the impact of your actions, expressing genuine regret, and a commitment to change. These components make up the framework of a sincere apology, ensuring that it addresses the underlying cause of the problem rather than its symptoms. Rebuilding trust after a conflict requires continuing efforts at reconciliation. This involves taking consistent actions that align with your words, while demonstrating your commitment to repairing the relationship.

Rebuilding trust takes time, but it is possible when paired with commitment and sincerity. Apologies must be backed by tangible changes in behavior, thus reinforcing spouse's sense of security. This process involves patience and transparency, which enables both partners to feel secure in expressing their vulnerabilities. As trust is restored, communication avenues naturally open up, enabling deeper connections and greater understanding.

Active listening and emotional validation are essential for effective communication during sensitive and delicate moments. 1 Thessalonians 5:11 encourages, "Therefore, encourage one another and build each other up."(NIV) Active listening and emotional validation demonstrate to your spouse that you value and respect their feelings, while fostering an atmosphere of trust and mutual support. When you listen without judgment and affirm emotions, you reflect the love and grace that God extends to us.

Healing Through Communication

Reflect on a recent conflict where communication broke down. Identify the triggers that caused the breakdown and consider how you might apply the mentioned techniques to handle the situation differently next time. Put your ideas in writing and schedule a time to talk about them with your spouse. Focus the conversation on improving communication and rebuilding trust.

It takes work and intentionality to overcome communication breakdowns. Couples can resolve disputes more effectively by recognizing typical triggers, applying workable repair techniques, and maintaining open lines of communication. To mend relationship wounds and create space for fresh intimacy and trust, apologies and reconciliation are essential.

Chapter 5
Building Emotional Intimacy

Vulnerability is The Key to Emotional Closeness

Years ago, I watched a friend navigate the tumultuous waves of a new marriage. At first, the couple seemed happy; however, beneath the surface, a multitude of unspoken fears and hidden insecurities began to erupt. One day, while sharing a quiet moment, my friend confessed that opening up to her husband felt like being exposed naked to the world. Both spouses found vulnerability difficult, yet it became their greatest strength. This revelation was pivotal, highlighting the importance of vulnerability in achieving genuine emotional intimacy. Relationships are strengthened when spouses engage in open communication, sharing both the positive experiences as well as concerns and vulnerabilities.

In the Bible, vulnerability is not just an emotional concept, but a spiritual one. In *James 5:16*, it says, "Confess your sins to each other and pray for each other so that you may be healed."(NIV) This scripture speaks to the power of vulnerability, not just for emotional closeness but for spiritual healing. In marriage, this becomes even more profound, as it symbolizes a relationship where both spouses share their vulnerabilities with each other, much like we confess our weaknesses and sins before God.

Vulnerability begins with recognizing the role it plays in deepening connections. When you allow yourself to be transparent, exposing flaws and all, you invite your spouse into the dark secret places of your life. This openness develops trust and empathy, creating a bond that withstands life's trials. Sharing personal fears paves the way for greater understanding of who you are. Discussing past experiences that shaped your beliefs helps your spouse better understand your perspectives and reactions. When these vulnerabilities are handled with care it lays the groundwork for a connection marked by love and authenticity that is able to handle the test of time.

Just as Jesus invites us to surrender all to Him and trust Him (Matthew 11:28), in marriage, as you allow yourself to be vulnerable by surrendering your fears and trusting your spouse, you become stronger as one. This sacrificial love, modeled after Christ's love for the Church, forms the foundation of emotional intimacy in a marriage. As it says in *Ephesians 5:25*, "Husbands, love your wives, just as Christ loved the Church and gave himself up for her."(NIV) The act of giving yourself to your spouse reflects the divine love that calls us to trust one another deeply. Yet, the fear of being vulnerable is often an obstacle to bonding. The dread of judgment or rejection can keep walls firmly in place, preventing meaningful connection. To address this fear, incorporate hands-on activities that encourage vulnerability. Try weekly sessions where each spouse shares personal stories that foster open communication without judgment. Writing private letters is another useful exercise. Write down ideas or emotions that may be hard to put into words and allow your spouse to read them in front of you. Once you have read the letter, take a moment to burn or tear up the letter. This serves two purposes: 1) A symbolic representation of release, and 2) an unspoken promise that it will never fall into the wrong hands. You can strengthen your emotional connection and gain insights into each other's inner lives by sharing these letters which become a potent way to increase understanding and connection.

Building trust through vulnerability involves reciprocal sharing. When one spouse opens up, it sets the stage for the other to do the same. This reciprocal exchange strengthens trust that frames the backbone of emotional intimacy. Expressing needs and desires openly further enhances this trust. By clearly stating what you need from your spouse, you demonstrate faith in their ability to support you. This clarity fosters an environment where both spouses feel empowered to share without hesitation while reinforcing the process of openness and mutual understanding.

Weekly Vulnerability Sessions

It is easy to overlook the importance of scheduling time for emotional connection amidst everyday chaos. Setting aside a specific time each week to share with your spouse is one way to achieve this. These times guided by love and faith are the moments to gain comfort in being vulnerable an d listening to each other. It is helpful to begin with prayer before starting this time of connecting. Philippians 4:6-7 reminds us to "present your requests to God" and "pray about everything," including personal fears and emotional issues. By inviting God into your relationship through prayer, it provides a sense of secureness where both spouses feel safe and supported as deep feelings, thoughts and experiences are shared.

These sharing sessions can serve as a forum for discussing past traumas, personal anxieties, and feelings that may be difficult to express in day-to-day interactions. The biblical idea of "bearing one another's burdens" (Galatians 6:2) is consistent with vulnerability in marriage. Emotional ties are strengthened, and mutual trust and understanding are fostered when they embrace vulnerability. Given that the Bible exhorts us to love one another selflessly (Ephesians 5:25), this is especially crucial in marriage. You respect each other's experiences and develop a closer bond by making time to listen, talk, and grow together.

Spouses expose themselves to one another during vulnerable moments, which can occasionally be awkward. However, cultivating the kind of emotional intimacy that Christ seeks in marriage requires embracing vulnerability. Love "always protects, always trusts, always hopes, always perseveres," according to 1 Corinthians 13:7. When both partners are at their most vulnerable, they are exhibiting the selfless love that this verse describes. When both partners are committed to fostering love, tolerance, and understanding, it transforms your relationship from superficial discussions to more profound and meaningful interactions.

The love and trust that God calls us to exhibit in marriage are reflected in emotional vulnerability, which is a strength rather than a weakness. You invite your spouse into your world by letting them see you in your most vulnerable moments, just as Christ invites us into His despite our imperfections. This transparency facilitates the development of a relationship based on sincerity and concern for one another, which makes it simpler for both parties to feel emotionally close and trusting (Proverbs 3:5–6).

Emotional Intelligence in Marriage

In any relationship, but particularly in marriage, emotional intelligence is essential. It examines the energy of the moment and aligns with biblical teachings in a Christian's life, urging couples to actively listen, thoughtfully process their feelings, and respond in a way that embodies the patience and love Christ exemplifies for us.

Acknowledging and comprehending your own feelings, as well as recognizing and honoring your spouse's emotional state, helps you avoid miscommunications and cultivate an environment of empathy and respect in your marriage. Reacting to your spouse with compassion and understanding is a reflection of Christ's empathy for us. Romans 12:15 exhorts us to "joy with those who rejoice; mourn with those who mourn." By demonstrating empathy, you support your spouse through both happy and sad times, deepening your emotional bond.

A crucial element of emotional intelligence is self-awareness, which enables you to comprehend how your feelings affect your words and behavior. (We will discuss further in Chapter 12). This self-awareness is essential for marriage because it prevents disagreements from escalating and helps couples resolve conflicts more effectively. The Bible also exhorts us to be teachable and humble, two qualities that can be crucial for a marriage's emotional well-being. We are reminded in Ephesians 4:2 to "Always be humble and gentle. Be patient with each other, making allowance for each other's faults because of your love."(NLT)

Creating Safe Spaces for Sharing

Setting boundaries based on mutual respect and trust is crucial to creating an atmosphere where both spouses feel comfortable expressing their feelings. As this space is preserved, it is understood that what happens "here" is for the ears and heart of one another only. Protecting each other's emotional health in a marriage is a sacred duty. Proverbs 4:23 states, "Above all else, guard your heart, for everything you do flows from it."(NLT) You can demonstrate your commitment to caring for each other emotionally, just as Christ cared for His Church, by creating an environment where both spouses are free to express their thoughts and feelings. It is important to responsibly value the information shared by your spouse to maintain an open and vulnerable relationship. This duty encompasses both happy and disagreeable moments.

Empathy in Marriage

Developing emotional intimacy requires empathy. It involves not only understanding your spouse's feelings but also sharing in their experiences, both their joys and their struggles. Empathy necessitates a strong bond and the readiness to walk beside your spouse, as Christ exemplified. According to Hebrews 4:15–16, Jesus sympathizes with our frailties and extends grace and mercy when we are in need. This Christlike empathy in marriage cultivates a bond based on humility, compassion, and unwavering love.

A deeper emotional bond is promoted when empathy is incorporated into everyday interactions. It entails giving your spouse your full attention, considering their perspective, and acknowledging their feelings. We are urged to "be devoted to one another in love" (Romans 12:10 NIV). Respect each other more than yourself. This loyalty and respect create an atmosphere where both parties feel appreciated and understood while fostering the emotional connection that keeps a marriage strong.

Chapter 6
Navigating Conflict with Grace

TOO OFTEN IN MARRIAGE, couples find themselves repeating cycles. Picture a couple sitting across from one another at the kitchen table, their words sharp and tensions high. They have previously been here, circling the same problems without finding a solution. Amidst this conflict lies an opportunity for growth. Unfortunately, they cannot see it at the moment. Marriages will inevitably experience conflict, but how the conflict is responded to matters greatly. According to James 1:19, the Bible exhorts us to "be quick to listen, slow to speak, and slow to become angry."(NIV) This scripture emphasizes the importance of considering every word carefully when tensions increase. Conflicts in a marriage can be either constructive or destructive. While preserving respect for one another, constructive conflict keeps the focus on the current problems. It entails addressing issues collectively rather than in opposition to one another, which is consistent with the biblical teaching of unity: "How good and pleasant it is when God's people live together in unity!" (Psalm 133:1 NIV). On the other hand, escalation and personal assaults are frequently a part of destructive conflict. This may cause emotional scars that are hard to heal.

The first step to changing the way you handle conflict is recognizing patterns. Empathy and understanding are at the heart of constructive conflict resolution. It encourages partners to express concerns without worrying about negative consequences. Destructive conflict often causes resentment and entrenched positions by blurring boundaries that perpetuates these issues. By recognizing these behaviors, you can steer your conversations toward positive outcomes and promote an environment of cooperation and compromise.

Christ's sacrificial love for His Church is reflected in conflict resolution that upholds mutual respect and seeks understanding (Ephesians 5:25). By exhibiting this kind of love, couples can resolve disagreements amicably and humbly while simultaneously fostering a climate of collaboration and compromise.

Conflict Resolution Tools

To facilitate constructive dialogue, consider incorporating practical tools that help resolve conflicts and promote productive discussion. Using time-outs is a valuable tool for defusing tense situations. It shows wisdom and self-control to pause or use a prearranged signal to step away for a moment when emotions are running high. This pause is not an escape, but a chance to collect one's thoughts and return to the conversation with balance and clarity. Proverbs 14:29 reminds us: "Whoever is patient has great understanding, but one who is quick-tempered displays folly."(NIV) Returning with a new perspective can transform contentious arguments into productive discussions. It is essential to respect your spouse's need to step away from the situation. Allowing departure without pursuit is vital.

Even in times of conflict, it is critical to preserve understanding and respect for one another. It is lucrative to acknowledge your spouse's viewpoint. It entails accepting his/her point of view as legitimate, even if it is different from your own. Harmony can be maintained by agreeing to disagree on some issues. It is okay for some problems to remain unresolved. It demonstrates maturity and empathy by respecting different viewpoints without imposing a consensus. "If two men agree on everything, only one person is doing the thinking." (Johnson)

Another helpful strategy is to establish a regular "conflict resolution" time. This entails setting aside a specific time to discuss issues in a neutral and non-emotionally charged environment. By doing this, you allow for candid conversations free from the demands of urgency and make sure that the topic is not left unaddressed. This proactive strategy ensures continuous communication and prevents problems from escalating.

Conflict Resolution Worksheet

Worksheets on conflict resolution can facilitate conversations by providing an organized approach to addressing issues. These worksheets outline procedures such as identifying the problem, exploring possible solutions, and determining next steps. They act as a guide, preventing discussions from degenerating into pointless territory and keeping them concentrated on finding a solution.

Consider creating a worksheet or locate one to help direct your conversations during disagreements. Use it to pinpoint problems, explore potential fixes, and reach a consensus on next steps. To monitor progress and make any necessary modifications, review it regularly.

It takes a deliberate shift toward positive techniques and resources that improve understanding and communication to navigate conflict with grace. By using these strategies, you can transform disagreements into opportunities for growth and connection, therefore creating a marriage that endures despite challenges.

Turning Conflict into an Opportunity for Growth

Your approach to disagreements can change if you view conflicts as normal aspects of any relationship, rather than as threats to the relationship. According to Proverbs 27:17, "As iron sharpens iron, so one person sharpens another."(NIV) During heated arguments, we frequently have the opportunity to sharpen our moral stamina, listening comprehension, and empathy. We can uncover deeper problems and unresolved emotions through conflicts, which provide a chance to address issues more constructively. The seeds of possible progress are present in every conflict. Transformation is made possible by recognizing the root causes of problems. Consider conflict as an opportunity to address issues that may otherwise go unnoticed rather than as a destructive force. This viewpoint encourages you to approach issues head-on in an effort to uncover the underlying tension. You can increase empathy and fortify your emotional connection by discussing these discoveries with one another. The benefits of these investigations are significant. While leading to a deeper and more complex understanding of one another, receiving the benefits of conflict requires openness and patience. Uncovering some underlying sources of conflict may need the help of a professional.

It is simple to respond impulsively and emotionally rather than thoughtfully when there is disagreement. But by stepping back, you can gain insight from these experiences. Important insights into your emotional landscape can be gained by thinking back on your own triggers and reactions. Every debate presents an opportunity to explore why specific subjects evoke more intense emotions. Gaining awareness of these triggers helps you better define your own needs and boundaries which may result in healthier future interactions. Discussing how things could be handled differently the next time encourages a more deliberate approach to future discussions, turning potential pitfalls into opportunities for personal growth and improvement.

The dynamics of your relationship may improve as a result of conflict. After settling a disagreement, consider establishing new objectives for your relationship that take into account the knowledge you have gained. These objectives include improving your communication skills or spending more time on activities that deepen your relationship. Conflict often highlights areas where communication styles need to be adjusted. By developing expressive (non-violent, non-hostile) strategies for thoughts and feelings, groundwork is laid for future interactions that are more productive in achieving resolution and change.

To reinforce constructive change, it is essential to celebrate progress made through conflict. Recognizing the strides you have made in resolving disputes gives you more confidence to face obstacles together in the future. To document your conflict management journey, consider starting a journal. Writing down your accomplishments and lessons learned serve as a reminder of your progress and offer concrete proof of your development. My *Couples Prayer Journal for Husbands & Couples Prayer Journal for Wives* is an excellent tool for tracking the growth of your relationship throughout the year. Expressing gratitude to your spouse for the resolution process strengthens your bond and validates the work both of you have put into keeping the peace. Respect and love are fostered when spouses show gratitude for one another's willingness to participate positively and actively.

Keep in mind, as you resolve conflicts with this perspective, that growth is not linear. Although there will inevitably be obstacles and setbacks, every advancement strengthens and makes the relationship more resilient. Recognizing that every disagreement can lead to a stronger bond between you and your spouse, embrace every opportunity for growth and development with bravery and curiosity.

By using this strategy, conflict in your marriage becomes a catalyst for positive change rather than a source of stress. It turns into a crucial aspect of your journey together, profoundly influencing both you and the relationship. Rather than avoiding or fearing conflict, accept it as a teacher that leads you to deeper intimacy and understanding with your spouse.

It takes practice and intentionality to integrate these viewpoints into your marriage. It entails changing the way you view difficulties and accepting them as opportunities for growth rather than as obstacles to be overcome.

You will discover that disagreements no longer have the same influence over your relationship as you proceed along this path. By handling disagreements with empathy and candor, you can establish a space where both spouses feel appreciated and understood, and where differences are celebrated rather than feared. Conflicts no longer serve as a source of division but rather as chances to strengthen bonds and promote respect for one another. Making the relationship more resilient, this method not only fosters personal development but also reinforces your marriage's foundation to life's inevitable challenges. By doing this, you develop a bond that endures through all stages of life and is based on love, trust, and understanding. In your marriage, conflict can become an ally, a chance for change that leads to a closer bond and more enduring fulfillment.

Setting Healthy Boundaries During Disagreements

In a marriage, boundaries are invisible lines that safeguard your emotional health in the event of conflict rather than presenting as obstacles to love. Because "everything you do flows from it" (Proverbs 4:23), the Bible exhorts us to protect our hearts. By giving you the room to process emotions without feeling overburdened, boundaries help you avoid emotional overload. These principles maintain mutual respect and recognize the dignity of both partners, encouraging each person to acknowledge the other's distinct qualities even when disagreements arise. They are designed to ensure interactions are conducted respectfully and safely without restricting participation. Setting these limits is crucial for maintaining emotional well-being and fostering more peaceful communication. Establishing boundaries aligns with biblical teaching found in Philippians 2:4 which reminds us to "look not only to our own interests, but also to the interests of others."(NIV) This scripture highlights the importance of respecting each other's emotional boundaries and creating an environment where both partners can express themselves freely without worrying about causing harm to one another.

Communicating boundaries clearly requires planning and accuracy, which involves setting specific verbal limits ahead of any potential conflict. Discuss with your spouse what is appropriate and what is not. This proactive dialogue fosters a common understanding and reduces the likelihood of miscommunication during tense situations. Listening and recognizing when boundaries are being pushed is essential to understanding and respecting one another's limits. It involves drawing a mutually respectful map of the relationship terrain that both partners can safely traverse without worrying about intruders. This understanding fosters a relationship where both parties feel respected and safe.

It can be challenging to uphold these boundaries during heated arguments though. Emotions may cloud judgment and lead to crossing boundaries. Using a safe word or signal can immediately halt actions and reinforce limits, allowing both parties to pause and reassess. Maintaining emotional control can be facilitated by engaging in self-regulation practices such as practicing mindfulness exercises or engaging in deep breathing. By keeping you rooted in the present, these techniques prevent you from acting impulsively and encourage more deliberate responses.

It becomes clear that boundaries need to be reviewed and modified as the relationship develops. Spouses can discuss changes in their needs during regular boundary check-ins. These discussions support adjustments, and allow boundaries to stay appropriate for the relationship over time. Flexibility in setting boundaries acknowledges that circumstances may change and previous arrangements may no longer be suitable for the current situation. Couples can strengthen their relationship and improve mutual understanding by adjusting to these changes together through candid communication.

Boundaries are dynamic; they change and grow with the relationship. They offer a structure that allows love to blossom without worrying about going too far or becoming too much. As you develop this habit, keep in mind that setting boundaries is an expression of love and respect that makes both spouses feel safe and valued in the relationship.

The Power of Forgiveness in Conflict Resolution

In any relationship, forgiveness is crucial. However, in marriage, where intimacy and trust are continually established and reestablished, it is even more essential. When Jesus tells Peter to forgive "seventy times seven" in Matthew 18:21–22, we are reminded that forgiveness is an ongoing process that releases both parties from the weight of past wrongs. Forgiveness is vital to restoring intimacy and trust in a marriage. It is not about forgetting the past or acting as though suffering never happened. Instead, it entails making the deliberate choice to let go of anger and resentment, releasing oneself from the weight of old grievances, and choosing peace (Ephesians 4:31-32). It is important to distinguish between forgiveness and forgetting, whereas the latter may never fully occur, the former is an ongoing process. Both spouses gain freedom when they let go of grudges, and make room for reconciliation and a fresh bond. This act of release opens the door for healthier interactions by enabling couples to move forward with empathy and understanding without endorsing harmful behavior.

Deliberate actions from both spouses is necessary to achieve true forgiveness. Make time to process your feelings and comprehend the impact of the situation on your heart. It is imperative that you acknowledge feelings of hurt and betrayal. Sincere reconciliation is made possible by this emotional clarity. A heartfelt apology is just as vital; it entails admitting wrongdoing and pursuing sincere reconciliation. A genuine apology establishes the foundation for forgiveness by expressing regret and demonstrating an awareness of the suffering caused. It conveys a desire to reestablish emotional closeness and trust, while creating an atmosphere in which healing can begin.

Forgiveness can impact the marital relationship in various ways. Couples can restore intimacy by releasing past resentments and building empathy and respect. Forgiveness reduces tension, helps spouses focus on the present, and promotes emotional well-being in their relationship.

Practical exercises can be beneficial in developing a forgiving mindset. Affirmations of forgiveness every day serve as gentle reminders of the strength that comes from letting go. Standing in front of the mirror and reciting phrases such as, "I choose to release resentment," or "I choose to embrace compassion and understanding" at the start of each day can help strengthen the resolve to forgive and cultivate an attitude that is receptive to healing and reconciliation.

Writing letters of forgiveness to each other is an additional exercise that can be used. Express your hurt feelings in these letters, but also acknowledge your desire to forgive and move on. By encouraging candid communication and fostering greater understanding, sharing these letters can enhance the relationship between spouses.

Chapter 7

Physical Intimacy and Connection

A Biblical Perspective to Rekindling Physical Intimacy

One evening, I received a call from a friend who confided that the fire in her marriage had dwindled, leaving her disheartened. This moment became a poignant reminder of how even the most deeply connected couples can sometimes lose touch with their physical intimacy. The Bible emphasizes the importance of physical intimacy as a symbol of love and unity within marriage. In 1 Corinthians 7:3-5, Paul advises couples to fulfill each other's needs, saying, "The husband should fulfill his marital duty to his wife, and likewise the wife to her husband."(NIV) The biblical perspective emphasizes mutual respect and understanding as the foundation of a thriving, intimate relationship. Revitalizing passion in marriage is attainable, yet requires a willingness to explore new experiences together, as a way of expressing the sacrificial love that mirrors God's love for His Church (Ephesians 5:25).

As we look at intimacy in this chapter, I invite you to relinquish the religious view that you hold regarding sex, intimacy and intercourse. For too long, these words have been taboo in Christianity, leaving the secular world to teach perverted messages about its purpose, thus causing deficits and unmet needs in Christian marriages.

God is Love (1 John 4:8 NIV). The more we know about God, the more we understand He desires to be intimate with us and to have continuous intercourse with us to build our relationship with Him. He continually expresses His love in all that He does for us, in us, and with us. He is the ultimate lover, and we were created in His image and likeness, as stated in Genesis 1:26. Similarly, within the confines of marriage, it is essential to understand the importance of maintaining continual intimacy and intercourse with your spouse to invigorate and strengthen the relationship.

Intimacy is defined as a close, familiar relationship characterized by emotional or physical closeness, trust, vulnerability, and mutual understanding.

There are four types of intimacy:

- **Emotional intimacy** is a feeling of closeness and connection in an interpersonal relationship.

- **Physical intimacy** is a form of intimacy that involves touch, cuddling, kissing, or sex.

- **Intellectual intimacy** is a form of intimacy that involves sharing ideas, opinions, interests, and knowledge with others.

- **Sexual intimacy** is a form of intimacy that involves sexual activity, intercourse, or orgasm.

Intercourse is defined as:

- Connections or dealings between individuals or groups

- An exchange of thoughts or feelings

- Physical sexual contact between individuals that involves the genitalia of at least one person

The journey towards deeper intimacy begins by acknowledging each other's unique needs while honoring shared commitments and valuing the person to whom you are connected. This is a testament to God's enduring design for marriage as both a divine covenant and earthly blessing. When marriage is viewed through these lenses, it creates a binding of soul and spirit that longs for more.

The goal in marriage is to maintain a strong and growing relational bond. Unfortunately, the fires of marriage do not always burn hot. Yet, there is hope. Enhancing romance often resides in the quiet power of small gestures. Capturing thoughts and feelings in tangible form by writing love notes or letters becomes a testament of affection. Your spouse's heart may be warmed again by a simple message that serves as a reminder of your enduring love. In addition to offering opportunities to reconnect and enjoy each other's company, surprise date nights can help break up the routine of everyday life. A spontaneous picnic beneath the stars or an unexpected trip to a place that holds special meaning for you both are examples of acts that demonstrate care and attention, cultivating an atmosphere where romance thrives. These small acts of love echo the Song of Solomon in which the couple expresses their love through heartfelt gestures and poetic language.

Engaging in shared activities can reignite the fire that once burned hot. Imagine enrolling in a pottery class together. The creativeness of shaping clay is analogous to the development of your relationship into something special. Engaging in a culinary adventure where you cook together and the kitchen becomes a place of literal and symbolic warmth, can also enhance your bond through flirtation, laughter, and exploration. These shared experiences strengthen the marital bond and produce joyous memories. Rekindling the fire requires spending time engaging in common interests or discovering new ones. The Bible encourages this practice in Ecclesiastes 4:9, "Two are better than one, because they have a good return for their labor."(NIV)

Open Communication

Intimacy requires open communication about desires and boundaries. According to Philippians 2:4, "Let each of you look not only to his own interests, but also to the interests of others."(NIV) The Bible emphasizes the value of respecting and honoring one another. Establishing a safe environment for discussing physical needs and desires ensures that both spouses feel heard and understood. Expressing desires in a non-judgmental manner promotes an atmosphere of acceptance and mutual respect. A deeper physical and emotional connection is made possible when both spouses are at ease discussing their needs and desires without worrying about being judged or rejected. This transparency promotes intimacy and inquiry, ultimately enhancing overall relationship satisfaction.

Incorporating love gestures throughout the day builds anticipation and excitement around intimate encounters which adds an element of thrill to the relationship. Include love notes, flirty texts, quick love calls, favorite fruits in lunch boxes, gentle caresses during dinner, inconspicuous pocket play, and lunch rendezvous (with your spouse) to heighten excitement and anticipation. Use your imagination. Be creative. Intimacy should not start when the door closes, and the lights turn off. These playful messages remind your spouse of your affection and desire thus building suspense and eagerness for intimate moments. Scheduling intimate encounters can also be beneficial, as it creates a sense of occasion that elevates the experience beyond mundane routine. Intimacy is enhanced by anticipation, which transforms routine moments into passionate and meaningful ones. It enriches the emotional tie, knitting your bond tighter than ever.

Cultivating Intimacy

Reflect on your current approach to intimacy within your relationship. Consider areas where you might introduce new experiences or gestures to enhance connection. Discuss these reflections with your spouse to explore opportunities for growth and deeper intimacy together. Create a shared bucket list of experiences, dreams, and aspirations that can rekindle embers of desire and connection. By embracing these ideas, you ignite passion and explore uncharted areas of intimacy in your relationship while creating a greater capacity for discovery. In nurturing the relational bond in this way, you cultivate a relationship that thrives on shared experiences, thoughtful gestures, open communication, and anticipation. These practices transform physical intimacy into a lively celebration of your love and dedication, reflecting God's intention for marriage and Christ's love for the Church, rather than merely existing as a component of marriage.

Understanding and Overcoming Intimacy Issues

Physical intimacy is a vital component of marriage, yet it often faces obstacles that seem insurmountable. Intentionality is necessary for intimacy. Stress and fatigue stand as primary inhibitors which drain energy and diminish desire. The demanding pace of life, family responsibilities, and long work hours can leave couples too exhausted for intimate connection. Intimacy is often neglected as a result of this exhaustion, leading to a growing distance between spouses. Rest is necessary to sustain both physical and emotional intimacy. Reassessing priorities and making an effort to set aside distraction-free time for relaxation and reconnection are two strategies to combat this. The Bible teaches in Matthew 11:28: "Come to me, all you who are weary and burdened, and I will give you rest."(NIV)

Another common barrier involves body image issues which affect confidence and self-perception. It can be challenging to fully participate in intimate moments without feeling self-conscious because of the feelings of inadequacy exacerbated by the media's portrayal of idealized bodies. These obstacles, if ignored, can cause the distance between you and your spouse to grow. However, the Bible affirms our intrinsic value in Psalm 139:14, "I praise you because I am fearfully and wonderfully made."(NIV)

Intentional action is necessary to address physical challenges. Establishing a calming nighttime routine can be a game-changer. You can escape the stresses of everyday life and enter a more private space by scheduling time to relax together at the end of the day. Consider dimming the lights, playing soothing music, sharing a warm bath, or giving a full-body massage. These simple acts of relaxation signal to your body that it is time to shift focus from external pressures to personal connection.

For more persistent physical barriers, seeking professional help is vital. Health conditions like chronic pain or hormonal imbalances can significantly impact intimacy. Seeking advice from a medical professional can lead to successful therapies that enhance your intimate life and restore balance.

Emotional barriers and earlier life traumas often intertwine with physical intimacy issues. Unresolved emotional conflicts can create an unspoken tension that prevents closeness and intimacy. Building emotional trust through open communication is key to overcoming many of these barriers. Address any underlying conflicts that may be hindering your connection by taking the time to discuss your feelings openly with your spouse. This dialogue requires patience and empathy, for both partners to feel safe and understood. For deep issues, consider seeking professional counseling.

Other barriers to physical intimacy that are rarely discussed within the Body of Christ, but have gained strong footholds in silence, are pornography and masturbation. They are seldom discussed openly, but they affect a multitude of men and women within the body. Both have a spiritual component.

Masturbation is the pleasing of oneself sexually without the engagement of "another," (your spouse). There are mixed opinions about masturbation. However, there is a spiritual aspect where masturbation can take on a life of its own, creating excessive and compulsive behaviors that become difficult to control. Because it was not God's design to meet the sexual needs of an individual by pleasing oneself, it interferes with the role and connectivity of the spouse. Further, the sensitivity of the sexual organ can be affected over time.

Masturbation has become a glorified way of abstaining from sexual engagement outside of marriage. Eliminating the need to bring the body and mind under subjection opens the door to issues later in a marital relationship.

Pornography, much in the same way as masturbation, has a spiritual component that comes alive. Initially, pornography may seem harmless, yet it creates arousal through mental imagery and desires in the body that cannot be fulfilled. Pornography has drug-like effects on the body and can increase desire for continued consumption. The sexual appetite grows for picturesque behaviors and positions that are unable to be satisfied by one's spouse. Therefore, disconnection and dissatisfaction occur in the spouse who is engaging in the pornography, and disconnection, rejection, and frustration occur in the spouse who is unable to fulfill the desires of the partner.

Through open communication, prayer, counseling, transparency, and accountability, barriers can be overcome. Consider setting aside a specific time each week to explore issues affecting the intimacy in your relationship. It will not only strengthen your connection but also create a resolve to face challenges together. By resolving conflicts, you create a foundation where physical intimacy can thrive without the weight of unresolved issues.

Numerous tools and resources are available to help individuals overcome intimacy challenges. Sexual health workshops and books offer helpful tips and techniques for improving physical intimacy. These resources provide professional viewpoints that can highlight areas for growth and improvement. Couples counseling services also provide a safe environment for discussing intimacy concerns with the assistance of expert supervision. A counselor can help identify trends and provide personalized strategies to enhance your relationship.

Understanding physical intimacy as a spiritual action adds another layer of depth to your relationship. Intimacy transcends the material world when it is regarded as a manifestation of divine love. This viewpoint encourages you to approach intimacy with intentionality and reverence, acknowledging it as a sacred act that brings you together on many levels.

Shared faith enhances the sexual relationship by providing a common framework of values and beliefs that fosters mutual understanding and respect. Engaging in spiritual discussions about intimacy allows you to explore how your faith informs your connection. Your relationship is strengthened as a result of these discussions which help both parties better understand one another's viewpoints on physical love. Praying together for a fulfilling intimate connection invites divine guidance into this sacred part of your relationship, consequently reinforcing your commitment to love each other fully and unconditionally.

The Spiritual Aspect of Physical Union

Physical intimacy, seen through a spiritual lens, brings a deeper dimension that can profoundly enrich a marriage. It becomes a way to connect on a spiritual level by transcending the physical and touching the divine. According to the Bible, a husband and wife's physical union is a reflection of their unity in Christ. This viewpoint encourages you to view your spouse not only as a friend but also as a spiritual equal, someone with whom you have a deep connection that reflects the love of the Creator as stated in Genesis 2:24 "That is why a man leaves his father and mother and is united to his wife, and they become one flesh."(NIV) In this context, physical intimacy turns into a sacred dance that reflects the divine and a celebration of unity.

Incorporating prayer or moments of silence before intimacy can deepen this spiritual bond. By aligning your intentions and focusing your thoughts, these techniques help you create a peaceful, connected space. They serve as a bridge bringing divine presence into your union and connecting the physical act to a greater purpose. It inspires you to treat every interaction with respect and appreciation while acknowledging the gift of connection that has been given to you.

Faith plays a pivotal role in enhancing sexual intimacy while providing a shared foundation that strengthens the relationship. You can gain a deeper understanding of how faith influences your relationship by exploring each other's values and beliefs through spiritual conversations about intimacy. This portion of your shared faith journey becomes another source that builds strength and resilience consequently grounding your relationship in love and understanding.

Marriage's physical union celebrates the unity that transcends the tangible world and reflects spiritual oneness. This union is a reflection of your dedication to the divine purpose that brought you together. Celebrating anniversaries as milestones of unity provides an opportunity to reflect on this journey, and acknowledges the growth and development that have occurred along the way. These celebrations serve as reminders of the love that has sustained you through challenges and triumphs, reinforcing the bond that continues to deepen with time.

Aligning your physical environment with your spiritual beliefs and turning them into a haven for connection is the first step in creating a sacred space for intimacy. Limiting the space to activities that honor the sacredness of intimacy further enriches this environment, by inviting divine presence into every encounter. Whether through shared prayers, singing songs, or sitting quietly together, these habits create a sense of reverence and intention that elevates your intimate moments.

Through these efforts, physical intimacy becomes more than an aspect of marriage; it transforms into an expression of love, faith, and commitment that enriches your relationship on every level. This practice invites you to engage with each other more deeply while exploring new dimensions of love and commitment that reflect the divine purpose of your union. As you continue to cultivate this sacred space within your marriage, you will find that your relationship grows in strength and depth, sustained by the shared spiritual journey that shapes your lives together.

This nurturing environment creates a platform for ongoing growth and transformation within your relationship. It encourages both spouses to explore individual spirituality while supporting each other's personal journeys. Through this shared exploration, a foundation is built grounded in love and faith that withstands life's challenges with grace and resilience. By embracing these practices wholeheartedly, you invite lasting fulfillment into your marriage in every aspect and discover new depths within yourselves as individuals as well.

Creating Habits of Physical Connection

Little acts of connection, made during the quiet times of everyday life, can create an intimate tapestry that fortifies your marriage. Developing regular physical connection routines, such as kisses or hugs to start the morning, helps you stay grounded and present. Despite their simplicity, these actions hold the power to create a positive atmosphere throughout the day. They serve as a reminder that you are each other's safe space amidst life's chaos. As a way to unwind after a long day, taking evening walks or holding hands while talking to each other can provide gentle moments to reconnect. These dedicated times encourage open communication and renewed commitment.

Being intentional about scheduling weekly date nights turns ordinary evenings into romantic escapades. These events become treasured customs that provide a welcome respite from the stresses of daily life, allowing the opportunity for undivided attention. Developing this pattern brings excitement and joy into your relationship, whether it is trying a new activity together or dining at your favorite restaurant. Similarly, exchanging weekly massages provides a tactile way to communicate care and attention. Massages not only soothe physical tension but also deepen emotional closeness and create intimate moments that remind each spouse of a cherished place within the relationship.

When time is limited, a quick kiss, a gentle touch, or a shared smile can help close the distance. Making intimacy a priority in your daily schedule ensures that it remains at the center of your relationship rather than an afterthought. Learning to engage with one another in close, nurturing ways without the result always being sexual intercourse, strengthens the relationship and builds resilience for times when sexual intercourse is not possible. This proactive approach signals that your bond is invaluable, deserving of time and effort regardless of external pressures. By prioritizing these practices, you safeguard the strength and depth of your connection.

Establishing and upholding healthy routines gives your marriage a rhythm that provides consistency and stability. They become touchstones that give you comfort and assurance while you navigate the uncertainties of life. By engaging in these activities, physical intimacy becomes an integral part of your emotional and spiritual connection that transcends its physical boundaries. Physical intimacy turns into a language for everyday expressions of love, strengthening the bond that underpins your marriage.

Sexual Intimacy - A Cornerstone

God, in His infinite wisdom, created sexual intimacy to be enjoyed within the confines of marriage as an expression of love between a husband and wife. It was designed to be a pleasurable experience for both spouses. For generations, women have been taught to believe that sex is to meet the needs of men. This thought process is erroneous. When considering the thousands of nerve endings in the genital areas alone, we understand that God had bigger plans than just meeting men's needs or being fruitful and multiplying. He wanted sex to be mutually enjoyable within the marriage covenant for both partners. Maybe even a little more enjoyable by women than men, in that He provided the clitoris for no other purpose but for her pleasure in achieving orgasm (O'Connell). The body is full of nerve endings and receptors. However, there is a high concentration in the genital area. In the penis and genital area, there are between 4,000 and 8,000 nerve endings and receptors; and in the vagina, there are between 8,000 and 12,000 nerve endings and receptors, with the greatest concentration in the clitoris. In further consideration of the various erogenous zones in both males and females and the sensory pathways involved in the sensitivity of the genitals, we understand the value the Creator placed on enjoying intimacy and sexual relations within marriage. It can be concluded that sexual intercourse is a divine design.

Passion grows when spouses explore each other's bodies with care and curiosity. Find comfort in the gentle exploration of your spouse's body. Get to know it like a detailed road map. If you don't know where you are going, then you can't get there. This can involve gentle caresses, soft massages, or exploring erogenous zones that may not have been fully discovered before. Taking the time to feel and understand each other's responses truly creates a deeper connection, not only physically but also emotionally. It also involves touching and kissing in places that are less commonly explored, like the back of the neck, wrists, or inner thighs, which can create heightened sensations and deepen the sense of closeness. The next time you engage in sexual intimacy with your spouse, leave the light on and open your eyes. Allow the vision of your spouse's pleasure to be etched in your mind and intensify the enjoyment of the experience. The Bible encourages husbands and wives to delight in one another's physicality as part of their oneness. In Song of Solomon, the bride and groom praise each other's bodies as beautiful and worthy of admiration: *"How delightful is your love, my sister, my bride! How much more pleasing is your love than wine, and the fragrance of your perfume more than any spice!"* (Song of Solomon 4:10 NIV). This encourages a healthy exploration of each other's bodies with respect and admiration, recognizing that the physical connection is holy and reflects God's design for marital love. As you explore, ask God to help you discover the secret treasures that He has hidden for discovery by lovers. The G-Spot and the P-Spot really do exist. Gentle exploration leads to discovery.

The gift of foreplay invites both spouses to be a part of the encounter. Too often, husbands reach climax and achieve an orgasm before their wives have achieved necessary lubrication or reached the level of intensity needed for her also to achieve orgasm in the midst of the engagement. Consequently the wife is left unfulfilled and feeling left behind. Foreplay is crucial in setting the stage for a meaningful and intimate connection. It is a time when you engage in physical touch, verbal affection, and external intimacy that ignites the body's arousal system. Proverbs 5:18-19 encourages us to find delight in one another and take pleasure in the physical aspects of marriage: *"Let your fountain be blessed, and rejoice in the wife of your youth...Let her breasts fill you at all times with delight; be intoxicated always in her love."*(NIV) This passage highlights the importance of joy and satisfaction within the marriage relationship. Foreplay, when done with love and care, can deepen the emotional connection between you while making you more responsive to physical and spiritual intimacy. Foreplay allows both to feel desired and connected, making you more responsive to each other's needs. It is not just about the result; foreplay is a way to savor the moments, to communicate desire and affection, and to create an atmosphere of emotional safety and connection. Engaging in activities such as kissing, touching, whispering affectionate words, and exploring each other's bodies can help build excitement, anticipation, and trust.

When was the last time you were home alone, turned your phones off, closed the blinds, and spent the day lying around in the nude with your spouse? Adam and Eve walked in the garden naked before sin came in and brought shame. It is time to remove the shame and once again have "foreplay in the garden".

Mind and Imagination

In therapy sessions, I frequently remind my clients, "Sex begins in the kitchen." This is a literal and figurative statement. They often take it literally and chuckle as they wonder, "What kind of freak is she?" As I go on to help them understand that once the concept of sex and intimacy is removed from the box of the bedroom, it takes on new meaning. Let us explore this a little deeper. Take a moment and see your mind as the kitchen of your body. In the physical kitchen, things come to life, meals are cooked, lunches are prepared, cakes and cookies are lovingly made for the family, and dinner is shared and enjoyed together. What comes from the kitchen has a positive or negative impact on the house as likewise, with the mind; thoughts originate, imaginations materialize, and plans develop that positively or negatively affect the emotions and responses of the entire body.

What are the thoughts that you have towards your spouse? How do you see him/her before you ever come close? Do you imagine your spouse in your arms? Can you see yourself kissing or caressing the body slowly? Can you imagine the taste and softness of your spouse's lips or see his/her naked body in your mind's eye? The mind and imagination that God has given humanity are powerful tools that play a vital role in intimacy with your spouse. Contrary to how some Christians have been taught to believe, having these thoughts about your own spouse is not lust or sinful. It enhances the sexual experience and helps reach orgasm, which is the targeted destination.

Climax and orgasm are natural expressions of sexual connection, but they should not be viewed as the sole purpose of the sexual encounter. Instead, they are a beautiful culmination of building physical, emotional, and intellectual intimacy. The Bible affirms the beauty of physical intimacy within the confines of marriage. In 1 Corinthians 7:3-5, it says, *"The husband render to his wife the affection due her, and likewise the wife to her husband…Do not deprive one another, except perhaps by agreement for a limited time, that you may devote yourselves to prayer; but then come together again, so that Satan may not tempt you because of your lack of self-control."* (NIV) This passage highlights the significance of mutual sexual satisfaction in marriage. Both spouses should strive to meet each other's needs, fostering a sense of unity and happiness. Understanding that sexual satisfaction comes from deep connection, not just physical release, is key. Both spouses should communicate openly about their needs thus learning what brings pleasure to the other, and remembering that patience is key. The act of building up to climax should be slow and intentional, allowing each spouse to enjoy the gradual increase of sensation and excitement. This might include changing the pace, introducing varying types of touch, or experimenting with different positions to find what feels most intimate and fulfilling. Guide your spouse so they know what feels good to you and what does not. Respond to them, whether with words, gestures, moans, or gentle hand placement. No one knows your body like you; teach your spouse how to ignite your passion.

Sensual Ideas to Build Intimacy

Sensual Touch Slow, intentional touch is a powerful way to create anticipation and heighten sensitivity, effectively conveying love and affection.

Intimacy, trust, and tenderness are all enhanced by a gentle touch on the face, a long-lasting kiss on the collarbone, or a soft stroke along the arm. Taking the time to be aware of your spouse's responses allows you both to experience the joy of touching without the pressure to rush toward climax.

Verbal Intimacy Whispering loving words, expressing appreciation for your spouse's body, or sharing thoughts about your connection can enhance the sensuality of the moment. Positive affirmations improve self-esteem and enhance emotional connection that leads to a more satisfying physical experience. Proverbs 31:29 speaks about a woman who her husband praises, *"Many women do noble things, but you surpass them all."* (NI) Complimenting and affirming each other's beauty, worth, and value within the marital relationship fosters a positive and intimate atmosphere that allows both spouses to feel cherished and loved.

Atmosphere Setting the scene for romance involves creating the ideal ambiance. Setting the mood for exploration and encouraging relaxation can be achieved by dimming the lights, playing soothing music, or even using candles or essential oils. The kind of openness required for a satisfying sexual relationship is fostered in a relaxed and secure setting.

Visual Display Adorning oneself in lingerie, minimal clothing, or no clothing at all creates an opportunity for intimate expression. Allowing your spouse to look longingly at you and enjoying the sight of them doing so increases levels of satisfaction.

Being honest about fantasies, desires, and what feels good or bad can help reduce insecurities and allow both spouses to feel more relaxed and connected. Vulnerability in sharing desires and exploring intimacy together strengthens the relationship and reflects the oneness that God intended in marriage.

In a healthy sexual relationship, both spouses are equally involved in creating pleasure with open communication and a focus on mutual satisfaction. By being patient, acknowledging each other's needs and appreciating each other's bodies, a rich intimate relationship can be built that strengthens both physical and emotional connection. For assistance with flirting and building anticipation, see my book Light the Fire: Flirt Again after I Do.

Chapter 8

Financial Harmony in Marriage

Finances are among the top issues that affect marital relationships. As beliefs and perspectives merge, there are often clashes along the way. To help navigate the way, God provided guiding lights to illuminate the path. There were commands and principles that Jehovah God gave the Jewish people to adhere to throughout eternity that carried a blessing. The more knowledge and understanding we gain of these instructions, the more abundant our lives become.

Tithes are the giving of a tenth of your increase. In giving the tenth, the remaining ninety is blessed.

And all the tithe of the land, whether of the seed of the land, or of the fruit of the tree, is the LORD'S: it is holy unto the LORD. (Leviticus 27:30 KJV)

Bring ye all the tithes into the storehouse, that there may be meat in mine house, and prove me now herewith, saith the LORD of hosts, if I will not open you the windows of heaven, and pour you out a blessing, that there shall not be room enough to receive it. (Malachi 3:10 KJV)

First fruit – Rosh Chodesh (offering on the first day of the Jewish month – New moon)

That thou shalt take of the first of all the fruit of the earth, which thou shalt bring of thy land that the LORD thy God giveth thee, and shalt put it in a basket, and shalt go unto the place which the LORD thy God shall choose to place his name there. (Deuteronomy 26:2 KJV)

Honor the LORD with thy substance, and with the first fruits of all thine increase: (Proverbs 3:9 KJV)

Sowing & reaping Whatever you give or do is returned with multiplication.

But this *I say:* He who soweth sparingly will also reap sparingly, and he who sows bountifully will also reap bountifully. So let each one *give* as he purposes in his heart, not grudgingly or of necessity; for God loves a cheerful giver. (2 Corinthians 9:6-7 KJV)

Honoring the principles of tithing, first fruits offering, and sowing & reaping, brings spiritual alignment and a return on investment (ROI). This allows your financial vision to be rooted in a sure foundation.

Creating a Common Financial Vision

One evening, I received a call from a friend who was overwhelmed. She and her spouse were arguing about finances again. They both had dreams, yet their paths seemed to diverge at every financial decision they made. This scenario is familiar to many couples. Financial harmony can feel elusive, especially when individual desires clash with shared goals. Yet, creating a unified financial vision is not only possible but rewarding.

The value of marital unity is emphasized throughout the Bible. According to Ecclesiastes 4:9–12, "two are better than one," since they receive a good reward for their efforts. The same is true for money. A couple grows stronger when they come together to have a common goal for their financial future. The first step in establishing common financial objectives is having an honest discussion about kingdom giving.

Discussing long-term goals, such as retirement planning or saving for a home, is essential. These discussions help identify common goals that serve as the cornerstone of a solid business alliance. A spirit of cooperation and stewardship is also fostered by adopting short-term objectives such as debt repayment or vacation budgeting, which promote unity and shared purpose.

Balancing Personal and Joint Priorities

It takes tact and compromise to strike a balance between shared and personal priorities. It is essential to recognize that both of you may have distinct financial objectives such as saving for interests or hobbies. Honoring these desires while also committing to joint expenses, such as vacations or educational funds, can be a delicate process. According to Philippians 2:3, the Bible exhorts us to "do nothing from selfish ambition or conceit, but in humility count others more significant than yourselves."(NIV) Achieving this balance requires open communication about individual priorities and how they relate to the larger financial picture. It is simpler to negotiate financial waters together while attending to individual and group needs when humility and empathy are practiced. For example, it respects both individual and shared goals to agree to set aside a certain percentage of personal income for hobbies while also making joint contributions to a family fund.

Building a Unified Financial Vision

One of the most critical steps in achieving your shared vision is developing a financial plan. The importance of planning is demonstrated by Proverbs 21:5, which states, "The plans of the diligent lead to profit as surely as haste leads to poverty."(NIV) Establishing rea- sonable deadlines for reaching financial objectives gives inspiration and guidance.

Once again we apply Ecclesiastes 4:9-12 which tells us that "two are better than one," for they have a good reward for their labor. This principle also applies to finances. When a couple unites to share a vision for their financial future, they become stronger. Defining shared financial goals begins with open dialogue about what both spouses envision for the future. Having a clear timeline makes it easier to stay on course, whether you are saving for a new home or planning for retirement. It is crucial to discuss long-term aspirations. These conversations help reveal shared dreams that form the foundation of a strong financial partnership. Having a flexible plan enables you to adjust to life's unforeseen circumstances which is essential when family dynamics or career paths change. The vision stays in front of you when you use visual aids to make progress tangible and rewarding. You uphold the stewardship principle and strive toward a financially secure future by following through on your plans.

Creating a Budget Together

The foundation for marital financial stability is laid by knowing the fundamentals of budgeting. A budget is a tool for prudent resource allocation that helps you live within your means. Before making financial decisions, Luke 14:28 reminds us to "count the cost." Successful budgeting involves identifying fixed expenses, such as rent or mortgage payments, and variable expenses that fluctuate in amount. Categorizing spending into needs and wants is crucial; needs are essential, while wants enhance your life. Understanding and managing financial resources is critical, as the Bible encourages us to "be diligent to know the state of your flocks, and attend to your herds." (Proverbs 27:23 NIV)

In order to achieve financial harmony, a joint budget is necessary. Begin by compiling all relevant financial data, including income, debts, and current expenses. Transparency is essential, and both parties must participate freely in this process. This task can be made easier by using budgeting tools or apps that offer real-time tracking and analysis. These resources provide information about spending patterns that highlight areas requiring improvement. To free up funds for other priorities identify underutilized recurring subscription fees. While upholding collective objectives, allocating discretionary funds for personal use within the budget respects individual autonomy. This approach ensures that each spouse can pursue personal interests without endangering shared financial goals.

Overcoming budgeting challenges requires patience and adaptability. Even the most carefully planned budgets can be unraveled by unforeseen expenses. "Go to the ant, you sluggard; consider its ways and be wise!" is wise advice found in Proverbs 6:6–8. Building an emergency fund, exemplified by the ant, helps prepare for the unexpected and provides peace of mind. The ant stores up provisions in the summer and gathers food at harvest. It is important to engage in open discussions about spending habits that focus on compromise rather than criticism. Proverbs 15:1 encourages gentle communication in the adage, "A gentle answer turns away wrath, but a harsh word stirs up anger."(NIV)

Resolving Money Related Conflicts

Marital disputes over money frequently have deeper roots than the arguments on the surface indicate. Determining the underlying causes of these conflicts can have monumental results. Many couples enter marriage with differing ideologies and financial backgrounds. One spouse may have been raised in a home where saving money was valued highly, while the other partner was exposed to a more laid-back spending style. These foundational differences affect each person's perspective on the function of money in daily life and long-term planning. Understanding the reasons behind conflicts requires an awareness of the varied backgrounds involved. Tensions can also be made worse by emotional triggers associated with saving or spending. While some people find security in saving as much money as they can, others may use spending as a coping strategy when under stress. Knowing one another's financial background and emotional attachments to money can help reveal the root causes of recurring arguments.

Strategies that prioritize respect and understanding are essential for having productive financial conversations. Active listening techniques can significantly alter the course of conversations. When one spouse expresses concerns or aspirations, the other should fully concentrate on understanding those viewpoints without rushing to a response. Spouses feel heard and appreciated in this setting. This conversation is further improved by using non-confrontational language. By using phrases like "I'm concerned about our spending habits" rather than accusatory ones like "You never think about our budget," one can avoid defensiveness and encourage candid conversation. This subtle change in wording has the power to alter the tone of financial discussions and yield better results.

Finding compromise in financial decisions involves creative solutions that respect both your needs and desires. When faced with large purchases, agreeing on a middle ground can be effective. Perhaps one spouse desires a high-end appliance, while the other prioritizes savings. Exploring different options, such as purchasing a refurbished or open box product, can satisfy both parties. Another tactic that preserves shared financial stability while honoring individual autonomy is to divide discretionary spending equally between the two. Each spouse has freedom within predetermined limits when equal amounts are set aside for personal expenses, lessening the possibility of conflict over separate purchases. Prioritizing shared priorities and experimenting with solutions, such as a joint "wish list" for larger purchases, can also help defuse possible conflicts.

Despite their best efforts, couples occasionally reach a dead end where outside advice is required. Receiving professional financial counseling provides new insights and knowledgeable guidance tailored to your specific circumstances. Speaking with a financial advisor can help clarify complex financial situations and ensure your choices align with your long-term objectives. Attending financial workshops or seminars provides practical techniques for better communication and decision making which helps you manage finances with confidence. In addition to teaching valuable skills, these experiences have the potential to reignite cooperation and partnership.

When exploring methods for resolving money-related conflicts, it is important to recognize that disagreements are a natural part of any relationship. Ephesians 4:32 urges us to "be kind to one another, tenderhearted, forgiving one another, as God in Christ forgave you."(NIV) The key lies in approaching these challenges with patience, empathy, and a willingness to understand the underlying issues. Financial disagreements can be transformed into opportunities for growth and unity by fostering open communication and seeking mutually beneficial compromises. This change can be further enhanced by implementing strategies, such as holding a monthly "financial retreat" day, for thoughtful, relaxed conversations.

Financial Stewardship

Couples who want to manage their finances wisely and purposefully must have a solid understanding of financial stewardship. Fundamentally, financial stewardship is seeing money as a means, not an end, to achieve life's objectives. It requires a shift in mindset from ownership to caretaking, where you manage resources conscientiously. Psalm 24:1 reminds us, "The earth is the Lord's, and everything in it."(NIV) Acknowledging that all resources ultimately belong to God, encourages you to align financial decisions with your priorities and values by considering their broader effects. Good stewardship naturally leads to a sense of responsibility in tithing and charitable giving. You demonstrate compassion and thankfulness by setting aside a portion of your income to support ministry and causes that align with your values. You acknowledge that having money is a way to make a positive impact on the world around you.

Integrating these ideas into routine financial procedures is a necessary part of practicing stewardship in daily life. Making charitable contributions a regular part of your financial routine can be achieved by developing a giving plan. As a part of this plan, a certain percentage of your income is set aside for charitable purposes, therefore enabling you to regularly contribute. Researching and choosing charities can become a shared passion when both spouses participate, adding a collaborative component to the giving process. Making sustainability and ethical spending a priority helps you make purchases that align with your values and promote responsible resource management. Selecting goods or services from businesses that prioritize moral behavior demonstrates a commitment to stewardship that extends beyond short-term financial gain.

The goal of long-term stewardship strategies is to maintain ethical standards while guaranteeing financial stability and security. You can increase your wealth and support businesses that share your values by investing in socially conscious funds. These investments guarantee that economic growth benefits society by taking governance, social, and environmental factors into account. You can develop financial resilience while upholding your values by prioritizing these tactics. Regularly reviewing these investments can be rewarding and instructive, ensuring ongoing alignment with individual values.

The Bible promotes giving, wise choices, and a profound appreciation for God's provision. As a couple, when you approach your finances with a divine purpose, you align your financial objectives with your beliefs and values, which in turn releases blessings upon your household because of your financial stewardship.

To ensure that your finances reflect love, faith, and shared goals, the Holy Spirit will guide you in the biblical values of unity, wisdom, and generosity along this journey of financial harmony. By embracing the principles in this chapter, you will not only build a secure financial future but also strengthen your relationship, rooted in mutual respect and devotion.

Chapter 9

Balancing Individuality and Shared Goals

CHRIST'S LOVE CREATES A caring and affectionate atmosphere that fosters individual development and the flourishing of relationships. This atmosphere is where dreams are pursued together and obstacles are met with bravery and faith.

Consider these crossroads that many couples encounter in their journey of relationship maturity: 1) the quest to evolve personally without compromising the unity of their marital relationship, or 2) Inspiration of one spouse for personal development and purpose in contrast to the lack of motivation and aspiration to do or learn anything new by the other spouse.

Developing oneself is essential to building a strong marriage. Embracing individuality within the relationship not only strengthens your bond but also enriches your shared experience. As you navigate the currents of life together, you cultivate resilience and unity, ensuring your relationship thrives in the face of external influences. Individual development enriches the relationship by adding layers of depth and understanding. As the relationship matures, ideally, spouses grow emotionally and intellectually, developing new skills and hobbies that bolster their self-esteem and bring fresh energy to the relationship. Where there is no growth, complacency and stagnancy set in, and the relationship is impacted. God is continually doing a new thing, and it is springing forth; shall you not know it? (Isaiah 43:19)

A biblical view of personal development emphasizes the value of cultivating one's gifts while lovingly serving others. According to 1 Peter 4:10, believers are urged to "use whatever gift you have received to serve others, as faithful stewards of God's grace in its various forms."(NIV) Personal growth encompasses both self-fulfillment and using one's gifts for the benefit of others, including one's spouse. You are called to grow together in the context of sacrifice and mutual service as you grow individually. The dreams, gifts, and desires that God placed in you are connected to the purpose for which you were created.

A key component of personal development is the pursuit of lifelong learning. It encourages adaptability and curiosity, two traits that energize relationships. In addition to expanding your horizons, taking classes, attending workshops or watching videos centered around your interests can bring fresh viewpoints and discussions into your marriage. By encouraging one another to view obstacles as opportunities for learning rather than as barriers, these educational endeavors help develop a mindset necessary for growth. According to Proverbs 1:5, "Let the wise listen and add to their learning, and let the discerning get guidance."(NIV) Developing wisdom is crucial for both individual growth and the success of a marriage.

It takes careful planning to strike a delicate balance between marital responsibilities and personal growth. Time management strategies become crucial for balancing individual interests with shared commitments. Setting aside specified time slots for personal pursuits helps to prevent personal objectives from taking precedence over marital responsibilities. It is equally important to set goals for personal development that complement marital values. You can achieve a balance between individuality and togetherness by making sure your goals align with your marriage's shared vision. Because of the unity this alignment creates, both spouses can support one another's individual paths without feeling abandoned.

Providing a model of sacrificial love, Ephesians 5:25-28, proclaims that husbands are called to love their wives just as Christ loved the Church. Similarly, wives are encouraged to respect their husbands (Ephesians 5:33 NIV). These guidelines demonstrate the consideration and care that must be given to each other when juggling individual and marital objectives. The welfare of the whole takes precedence over individual interests while genuinely balancing the mutual consideration of each other's needs and growth.

To foster personal growth within a marriage, a supportive environment is crucial. By commemorating successes and milestones together, spouses can foster a supportive atmosphere. Acknowledging one another's development strengthens your relationship by reaffirming the importance of personal growth and mutual support. This supportive dynamic is further enhanced by providing constructive criticism on personal endeavors. Feedback should be given respectfully and empathetically, emphasizing possible enhancements rather than faults. By encouraging an environment of open communication, this strategy enables both spouses to develop personally and strengthen the bond. According to Proverbs 27:17, "As iron sharpens iron, so one person sharpens another."(NIV) Supporting and constructively critiquing one another's development makes you both better versions of yourself and improves your relationship.

Celebrating personal development and individuality within marriage is not merely an act of self-expression but a vital component of a healthy relationship. Also, encouraging personal style and expression allows each spouse to maintain a sense of identity within the union. Whether through fashion, hobbies, or interests, these expressions contribute to a richer, more diverse relationship. Supporting unique career paths and aspirations further enriches this dynamic. Encouragement in pursuing individual growth affirms each spouse's value beyond the role in the marriage and fosters mutual respect and admiration.

Embracing Diversity in Marriage

One lovely feature of marriage that reflects God's love and creativity is unity in diversity. Each spouse contributes distinct strengths and viewpoints to the partnership, making it richer and more dynamic. Couples can appreciate the special gifts each spouse brings by celebrating individual differences and unique qualities. While one spouse may enjoy quiet evenings at home, the other may be an extrovert who enjoys social events. By acknowledging and respecting these differences, creative ways can be discovered on how to enjoy both quiet evenings and social gatherings. By encouraging respect and understanding, this strategy not only values individuality but also fortifies the relationship.

As couples embrace one another's personal individuality, it is also of utmost importance that they consider each other's cultural differences as well. Marriages that blend diverse cultural backgrounds bring a richness that transforms the tapestry of life together. This diversity infuses relationships with new perspectives, traditions, and ways of communicating that can both enrich and challenge the marital bond. Understanding these cultural differences becomes crucial as one navigates the complexities of marriage. If not recognized, differences in communication styles can lead to misunderstandings. While one spouse may be direct and expressive, the other might value subtlety and indirectness. These variations require patience and an open mind to bridge the differences.

Similarly, different traditions and celebrations offer opportunities for learning and growth. Each spouse brings a rich history of customs that can be shared and celebrated together. These traditions might include specific holidays, rituals, or even daily practices that hold deep significance. By embracing these differences, couples can create a dynamic environment where both partners feel valued and understood.

The Bible acknowledges the diversity in human relationships and speaks to the beauty of different cultural and individual backgrounds. In 1 Corinthians 12:12-14, Paul describes the Church as the body of Christ, composed of many parts, each with a distinct role, yet all united in a single purpose. Similarly, in marriage, the blending of diverse backgrounds, cultures, and traditions can create a stronger, richer relationship.

Marriage is a place where both spouses bring their unique perspectives, and by embracing these differences, a couple honors God's creative diversity. As 1 Peter 4:10-11 suggests, each spouse should use individual gifts to serve one another and glorify God through the relationship. This biblical perspective encourages couples to celebrate their differences as a reflection of God's intention for diversity and unity.

Celebrating cultural heritage together is more than just acknowledging differences; it is a way to honor the past while building a future together and incorporating cultural traditions into daily life, such as sharing stories from childhood, favorite family recipes, or cooking traditional meals. These acts not only honor individual backgrounds but also enrich the shared life you are building. Celebrating cultural holidays and festivals together offers another layer of connection. Participating in these celebrations fosters respect and appreciation for each other's heritage.

Navigating cultural conflicts requires sensitivity and understanding. While these conflicts might arise from differing familial beliefs or practices, they also present opportunities for deeper connection. Engaging in cultural sensitivity training can provide valuable insights into one another's backgrounds consequently helping to dispel misconceptions and build empathy. Seeking advice from culturally diverse couples who have successfully navigated similar challenges can also offer guidance and support for your marriage.

Building a unified cultural identity involves creating something new from the rich tapestries of your individual backgrounds. This process respects both spouses' histories while forging a unique path forward. Creating new traditions that blend cultures can be a delightful exercise in creativity and compromise. Whether it is combining holiday celebrations or developing your own family rituals, these traditions symbolize the unity you share. Cooking meals from each culture together can be both an enjoyable and educational experience offering a tangible way to explore each other's backgrounds.

By embracing diversity within marriage, you create an environment where the celebration of differences is the goal, not just toleration. This approach fosters a sense of belonging and understanding that transcends individual backgrounds. As you navigate this complex landscape, remember that each challenge is an opportunity to deepen your connection and expand your horizons.

The journey of embracing diversity in marriage is one of discovery and growth. It requires openness to new experiences and a willingness to continually learn from each other. By valuing the richness that each culture brings, you can create a marriage that is not only resilient but also vibrant and fulfilling.

Understanding cultural differences and their impact on marriage involves acknowledging the unique perspectives and nuances that each person brings to the relationship. These differences might manifest in communication styles, decision-making processes, or even conflict resolution approaches. By recognizing these variations and addressing them with empathy, you pave the way for constructive dialogue and mutual respect.

Celebrating cultural heritage together strengthens the bond between spouses by creating shared experiences that honor individual backgrounds while building new memories together. Incorporating traditions into daily life enriches your relationship by fostering appreciation for each other's unique contributions.

Navigating cultural conflicts requires patience and understanding as you work through differences to find common ground. As a couple embarking on this journey of embracing diversity in marriage, newfound strength is discovered through understanding and appreciating each other's unique perspectives while creating shared experiences that honor individual backgrounds and building new memories together as one unified entity.

Through committing to understand each other, an environment is cultivated where love flourishes, despite all odds, in a relationship built on trust, respect, and a shared vision for what truly matters. Embracing individual differences is a testament to the enduring strength that arises when two individuals come together as one, while honoring their unique identities along the way.

Personal Development Exercise

Consider your most recent personal development experience for a moment. Think about the knowledge or abilities you have gained and how they have improved your life and marriage. Write down five personal goals, then identify three you wish to pursue over the next year. Ensure that your personal objectives for the upcoming year align with your marital values. Discuss these objectives with your spouse and explore how you can support each other in achieving your goals.

Improving oneself is only one aspect of fostering personal growth in a marriage; another is fortifying the bond between spouses. Maintaining a balance that respects both personal goals and marital commitments is crucial as you set out on your individual growth paths. To achieve this balance and ensure that each other feels appreciated and supported on the journey, it is important to be adaptable and communicate openly. The depth and resilience of the relationship are enhanced by maintaining an environment that values and promotes personal growth.

Keep in mind that every person's journey is different due to culture or experiences. Encourage one another by providing the space and encouragement needed to explore new interests and passions. Your marriage's foundation is strengthened by this reciprocal support, which also improves your personal lives. Allow time for personal reflection and sharing insights, thereby weaving personal growth into the fabric of your relationship.

As you navigate the complexities of balancing personal and shared goals, embrace the opportunities for learning and growth that arise along the way. In addition to strengthening your individuality, these experiences will also deepen your bond with your spouse, and foster a respectful and understanding marriage. A relationship built on these tenets is like a living thing, constantly changing, growing, and thriving with every stage of life.

Through these practices, a relationship is fostered in which both individual and shared dreams are nurtured, culminating in a relationship that is resilient and fulfilling. In this environment, love blossoms as both spouses continue to grow together, supporting one another through every stage of life's journey, making the marital bond not just a partnership but a thriving coalition of shared and individual ambitions. A marriage that fosters mutual respect and individual pursuits aligned with biblical principles creates a dynamic and fulfilling collaboration.

A Growth Mindset for Marriage

A growth mindset transforms how you perceive challenges and failures in your marriage. Psychologist Carol Dweck coined this concept based on the idea that intelligence and abilities can be developed through hard work and dedication. In the context of relationships, you should see challenges as opportunities for learning and growth rather than as insurmountable obstacles. When you encounter difficulties, you should view them as opportunities to improve, which in turn strengthens your relationship and personal resilience. Failure is not a finality, but rather a steppingstone to deeper connection and better understanding. This perspective encourages continuous improvement that fosters a dynamic and constantly changing relationship rather than a static one.

To cultivate a growth-oriented approach in your marriage, begin by setting joint learning goals. These goals include mastering new skills together, such as cooking a complex dish or learning a new language. The act of learning together not only builds skills but also strengthens the bonds between individuals. Encouraging each other to step out of comfort zones can lead to shared experiences that enrich the relationship. Whether it's trying a new hobby or tackling a challenging issue, supporting each other in these endeavors reinforces trust and partnership. This support creates a safe environment where taking risks is celebrated and failures are viewed as valuable lessons rather than setbacks.

Adopting a growth mindset is not without hurdles. Often, fear of failure and rejection can hinder progress. These fears may stem from past experiences or deeply ingrained beliefs about personal capabilities. Addressing these fears involves challenging limiting beliefs about oneself and the relationship, thus requiring a shift in perspective. By cultivating an environment of mutual support and encouragement, you dismantle barriers that restrict growth. Emphasizing open communication about fears and insecurities allows both spouses to confront these issues together, therefore transforming potential obstacles into opportunities for deeper connection.

Reflective practices play a crucial role in reinforcing a growth mindset. Journaling about personal growth experiences provides a space to process emotions and insights gained from various situations. This practice offers clarity and perspective, and allows you to track development over time. As you reflect on personal experiences, consider how they align with your relationship goals. This alignment ensures that personal growth supports the overall well-being of the relationship. Sharing these reflections with your spouse deepens mutual understanding and strengthens the bond between you. By embracing a growth-focused mindset, you create a marriage marked by resilience, adaptability, and intimacy.

The journey towards fostering a growth mindset in marriage is ongoing, and requires patience and commitment from both parties. It involves embracing change as an integral part of life and relationships, while recognizing that each challenge presents an opportunity for growth. By cultivating this mindset together, you build a marriage that flourishes on mutual respect and shared aspirations.

In this endeavor, remember that small steps lead to significant transformations. Consistent effort over time yields profound results that enhance both the individual and the relationship as a whole. As you continue to nurture a growth mindset within your marriage, you pave the way for lasting love and fulfillment, a love that adapts to life's changes with resilience and grace.

Chapter 10

Trust and Forgiveness

REBUILDING TRUST AFTER BETRAYAL

Betrayal is often thought to be only sexual infidelity. However, betrayal of trust can take various forms, including emotional, physical, and financial. Betrayal is any action that dishonors the marital commitment and damages trust.

Emotional Betrayal includes emotional cheating, withdrawing emotionally, engaging in verbal or emotional abuse, and pornography usage. According to Gottman, if your partner would be upset by the things you have shared or would be uncomfortable watching the interaction, then it is categorized as betrayal.

Physical Betrayal encompasses infidelity, affairs, and physical violence.

Financial Betrayal involves mishandling finances, hiding debts, or secret spending.

When trust is lost, a seemingly insurmountable gap is left behind. Imagine a couple seated in their living room; the atmosphere thick with hurt feelings and unsaid words. There is an unseen barrier between them because of the betrayal of one partner. A relationship's foundation is struck by betrayal, which is capable of causing a flurry of emotions that can make you feel as though you're in a never-ending downpour. It has a significant emotional impact. Brewing beneath the surface and tainting every encounter is anger and hurt which are frequently the first emotions to surface. Your confidence and sense of self-worth decline along with trust that leads you to doubt your own judgment and value. Every step forward feels like two steps back when trying to overcome resentment.

According to the Bible, trust is the cornerstone of every relationship. "Trust in the Lord with all your heart and lean not on your own understanding; in all your ways submit to Him, and He will make your paths straight." Proverbs 3:5–6 NIV highlights the value of having faith in God and can serve as a model for restoring trust in a marriage. The Lord's unfailing reliability provides couples with a model for their own restoration, whereas human trust may wane. Once lost, trust necessitates a strong belief in God's healing power as well as in one another.

Starting the healing process requires an understanding of the effects of betrayal. Because of the profound psychological damage it causes, both spouses must face the suffering and the feelings that accompany it. As you struggle with the changed dynamics of your relationship, feelings of inadequacy may emerge, which are exacerbated by anxiety and depression. Navigating these difficult places without losing sight of the love that once held you two together is the tricky part. The first step to recovery is admitting the betrayal and its effects. This entails facing the feelings head-on and giving each spouse room to communicate hurt and uncertainty. Here, Ephesians 4:26–27 provides guidance: "In your anger do not sin: Do not let the sun go down while you are still angry, and do not give the devil a foothold."(NIV) This teaching promotes addressing anger and betrayal before they fester and allow bitterness to take root.

Rebuilding trust necessitates a methodical strategy based on honest dialogue and shared dedication. Begin by acknowledging the betrayal and its ripple effects on your relationship. Validating one another's feelings and experiences is crucial. After the acknowledgement, discuss the incident openly and sincerely. The dialogue should be free of defensiveness or blame; instead, try to focus on understanding the underlying causes and emotions involved. It becomes essential to set reasonable and unambiguous expectations for the future. To promote a renewed sense of security and trust, both spouses must agree on the boundaries and behaviors that will guide future interactions. "Be devoted to one another in love. Honor one another above yourselves," as stated in Romans 12:10, applies to both building and rebuilding trust—that is, respecting one another's suffering, vulnerability, and desire to heal.

Creating a safe space for healing involves more than just words; it requires action and intention. Establish an environment conducive to rebuilding trust through regularly scheduled conversations dedicated to trust-building. These discussions provide an opportunity to address lingering doubts or concerns in a non-judgmental setting. Commitment to maintaining this open dialogue is vital, allowing both spouses to voice their needs and fears without fear of reprisal. This safe space encourages vulnerability, a crucial component in rebuilding trust and intimacy. It is not limited to formal interactions, but simple assurances, like a hug or a shared look; they can speak volumes in rekindling closeness. Psalm 3418 reminds us that "The Lord is close to the brokenhearted and saves those who are crushed in spirit."(NIV) This biblical truth highlights that even in brokenness, healing is possible, and God's presence can be felt in the process of healing relationships.

Practical exercises facilitate the restoration of trust by reinforcing positive interactions and shared experiences. By encouraging mutual reliance, trust-building exercises like trust falls or group projects can improve your relationship. These activities promote teamwork and mutual support which serve as physical manifestations of trust in action. Restoring confidence and security in the relationship can be accomplished gradually by setting modest, attainable trust goals. Celebrating these milestones reinforces progress and motivates continued effort.

Engaging in common interests not only brings happiness but also acts as a reminder of mutual strengths. Matthew 18:21–22 provides a helpful perspective on forgiveness that couples can use in the healing process. "Then Peter came to Jesus and asked, 'Lord, how often should I forgive someone who sins against me? Seven times?' No, not seven times," Jesus replied, but seventy times seven." (NLT) This passage highlights the importance of ongoing forgiveness in marriage and the gradual process of restoring trust.

The Process of Genuine Forgiveness

In a marriage, forgiveness is a profound and transformative act. It's about letting go of resentment and making the decision to move forward, not just about overlooking or forgiving a spouse's error. Forgiveness in a married relationship is not about condoning harmful behavior or pretending the past didn't hurt. Instead, it recognizes and acknowledges the pain. Condoning implies acceptance of the wrong, which forgiveness does not require. Instead, forgiveness permits healing without excusing behavior. Letting go of the emotional grip that old grievances have over you is a deliberate choice. It is a personal decision that allows you to reclaim your peace and emotional well-being. Making this decision is essential to moving forward because it releases you from the shackles of bitterness, allowing room for love and understanding to blossom once more. It is important to understand that as your spouse walks through the process of forgiveness, there are times that they may appear to regress and experience anger, hurt and pain all over again. Although they have forgiven, healing is a process.

In the Bible, forgiveness is not only a command but a divine principle that mirrors God's forgiveness toward us. Colossians 3:13 says, "Bear with each other and forgive one another if any of you has a grievance against someone. Forgive as the Lord forgave you."(NIV) When spouses forgive, they emulate the grace God extends to them, fostering a relationship of mercy and restoration.

Achieving forgiveness involves several intentional steps, each requiring introspection and empathy. The journey begins with acknowledging your personal pain without minimizing it. This acknowledgment is essential as it validates your feelings and underscores the significance of what has occurred. It's important not to trivialize your emotions or rush through them. Allow yourself to feel the hurt. Only by acknowledging the pain can you begin to heal from it. Next, strive to empathize with your spouse's perspective. This doesn't mean agreeing with their actions but understanding their motivations and circumstances. Empathy opens the door to compassion, by facilitating a more profound connection that aids in healing. Letting go of past grievances is the final and perhaps most liberating step. This release is not about forgetting but about freeing yourself from the emotional weight of those memories. It involves a conscious effort to focus on the present and future rather than dwelling on past pain. Matthew 6:14-15 emphasizes the importance of forgiveness: "For if you forgive other people when they sin against you, your heavenly Father will also forgive you. But if you do not forgive others their sins, your Father will not forgive you of your sins."(NIV)

Forgiveness, while liberating, is frequently hampered by seemingly insurmountable barriers. Since it can be intimidating to open your heart again after being hurt, vulnerability is a significant concern. Recognizing that there may be hesitation in offering forgiveness due to a fear of being hurt again, it is important to strike a balance between forgiveness and self-protection. It is about establishing healthy boundaries that safeguard your well-being while allowing space for reconciliation, grace, and growth. Overcoming these obstacles requires courage and commitment to personal development. You must trust in yourself and your capacity to heal, knowing that vulnerability also holds the power to deepen intimacy and connection. Proverbs 4:23 reminds us to "Above all else, guard your heart, for everything you do flows from it."(NIV) King Solomon encourages us to protect our hearts while practicing forgiveness and restoration. By embracing forgiveness with grace, couples can break free from past hurts while making room for renewed love, peace, and trust in their marriage.

Practical exercises can be beneficial in developing a forgiving mindset. One such activity is writing letters of forgiveness to one another. These letters provide both spouses with a space to express their feelings and intentions without interruptions. In these letters, express what has hurt you, and your desire to forgive and move forward. Reading these letters aloud can be a powerful act of vulnerability and connection. Another exercise involves practicing daily affirmations focused on healing. These affirmations strengthen your resolve to let go of past hurts and serve as a reminder of your ability to forgive. By gradually cultivating a more forgiving perspective, such practices help reorient attention from resentment to healing.

Keep in mind that every couple's journey toward forgiveness is different as you complete these exercises. Forgiveness is a process that develops at its own speed, influenced by readiness and unique circumstances. During the process have patience with both you and your spouse, allowing your feelings to fluctuate naturally as they undoubtedly will. With time, forgiveness becomes a gift you give not only to your spouse but also to yourself; it is a gift of peace, freedom, and renewed connection. A foundation for a relationship built on empathy, love, and understanding is created when both spouses sincerely and openly commit to this process.

Love grows new roots in this forgiving environment fostered by tolerance and kindness. Instead of acting as obstacles to intimacy, the scars from previous injuries serve as reminders of resiliency and personal development. When you forgive, your relationship becomes a place where hope and healing coexist, illuminating the way to a future free from the burdens of past transgressions.

Building Trust

Trust is the solid foundation upon which every thriving marriage stands. It serves as the bedrock of a relationship, enabling meaningful and profound connections between spouses. Intimacy becomes elusive, and the once-unbreakable bond may begin to wane in the absence of trust. Allowing yourself to be vulnerable and share your deepest feelings and thoughts without fear is only possible with trust. It opens the door to a real connection where both spouses are comfortable enough to express themselves fully. Love blossoms in its presence, nourished by the knowledge that your spouse will value and safeguard your life together.

Reaffirming your commitment to one another through consistent actions is necessary to build trust. Keeping promises and honoring commitments are fundamental practices that reinforce trust on a daily basis. When you say you will be there, and you are, or when you promise to listen without judgment and follow through, you demonstrate reliability. These actions create a pattern of dependability that strengthens the trust between you. It is in these everyday interactions that trust is either built or destroyed. Consistency in words and deeds fosters an environment where trust can flourish while providing a sturdy framework for your relationship.

Cultivating a trust-centered relationship requires intentional efforts. Regular engagement in trust-building activities helps maintain a strong connection. Engagement might include setting aside time for meaningful conversations or participating in activities that require cooperation and mutual support. These shared experiences reinforce your bond, reminding you (as a couple) of the strength that comes from unity. Setting joint goals further reinforces mutual trust as you work together towards shared dreams and aspirations. By aligning your efforts and supporting one another's ambitions, you create a relationship based on trust and mutual respect.

The benefits of a trust-filled marriage are manifold. When trust permeates your relationship, emotional safety and security become the norm. You both feel free to express yourselves without the fear of ridicule. This security enhances communication and allows open and honest dialogue about everything from mundane daily tasks to significant life decisions. In a marriage where trust thrives, collaboration becomes seamless. You work together towards common goals with confidence, and the knowledge that each partner is committed to the other's well-being. Trust acts as a catalyst, enhancing every aspect of your relationship.

Trust Milestones Chart

Create a chart to track your progress in rebuilding trust. Every milestone is a step closer to building a stronger relationship. Celebrate successes together using this chart to strengthen your resolve and reinforce your commitment to healing.

Every couple's journey to regain trust after betrayal is different. It demands patience, empathy, and dedication from both spouses as you navigate the complex terrain of restoration together. Practical exercises serve as tools to reinforce trust and provide tangible opportunities for growth and connection.

As you embark on this healing journey, remember that restoring trust is a gradual process marked by small successes and mutual understanding. Each step forward strengthens your bond, laying the foundation for a relationship that thrives on honesty, transparency, and mutual respect.

Maintaining Transparency and Accountability

Transparency forms the backbone of any thriving relationship. It is essential for sustaining trust between spouses. Imagine a couple sharing their deepest thoughts and feelings while walking on the beach. This scene depicts the essence of transparency through sincere communication void of hidden agendas or secrets. When you embrace openness, you create fertile ground for trust to flourish. Honesty allows each person to feel safe and know each one is valued and respected. Secrecy, on the other hand, creates suspicion and doubt which erodes the foundation of trust that holds a relationship together.

Developing accountability practices helps maintain crucial elements of a healthy marriage. Setting mutual goals for accountability can ensure both spouses remain committed to their promises. Whether it is financial responsibilities or daily chores, having clear objectives keeps both parties aligned and focused on shared values. Regularly reviewing these commitments fosters a sense of responsibility and reliability. It is important to have periodic check-ins where you can discuss progress and address any areas of struggle. By doing so, you reinforce a culture of accountability that strengthens trust.

A culture of honesty is paramount in fostering an environment where truthfulness is prioritized. Couples must encourage open dialogue about mistakes and missteps without fear of judgment or retribution. This openness fosters a safe space where spouses can acknowledge faults and work together towards a resolution. Celebrating honesty, even when it is difficult, reinforces the importance of transparency and accountability. When one spouse admits to a mistake, acknowledge the courage it took to do so. This acknowledgment fosters a deeper connection and mutual respect.

Tools that enhance transparency are invaluable in maintaining accountability within your relationship. Shared calendars can serve as practical aids to help you manage commitments, maintain transparency and schedule collectively. This tool also ensures both spouses are aware of each other's responsibilities. Financial accounts shared between spouses further exemplify transparency. Openness about finances eliminates potential sources of conflict and mistrust, fostering a cooperative approach to managing resources. Journaling offers another avenue for tracking personal growth and commitments. By documenting experiences and reflections, you gain insight into your progress and areas for improvement.

Tracking Accountability

Create a chart outlining your goals and commitments to each other. Utilize it to track progress, celebrate achievements, and identify areas in need of improvement. This graphic aid serves as a constant reminder of your mutual obligations and commitment to transparency.

Transparency and accountability are not mere concepts but active practices that require intentional effort from both spouses. Both characteristics form a dynamic interplay that strengthens the fibers of your relationship thus weaving together trust, honesty, and mutual respect. As you continue to cultivate these elements within your marriage, remember that they thrive on open communication, mutual understanding, and shared values.

Recognize that fostering transparency in your relationship is a continuous, daily process that requires both parties to be committed and dedicated. It entails respecting one another's boundaries while simultaneously being honest about feelings, ideas, and intentions. This balance creates an environment where trust can deepen over time and enhance emotional intimacy and connection.

The journey towards greater transparency may present challenges as you navigate vulnerabilities and fears of judgment. However, it is through these moments of openness that true intimacy flourishes. By embracing vulnerability together, you build a foundation of trust rooted in authenticity rather than pretense.

Accountability plays an integral role in sustaining this level of openness by ensuring that both partners remain committed to their promises and responsibilities. It serves as a constant reminder of the mutual dedication required for a successful relationship built on trust.

Although it requires deliberate effort, maintaining accountability and transparency in your marriage has significant benefits, including a stronger bond and greater understanding. As you engage in these behaviors regularly, you will discover that they become second nature as essential components of a thriving relationship marked by honesty and trustworthiness.

In this environment where transparency is valued above all else, love can flourish and establish solid roots grounded in truthfulness and integrity. The bonds forged through transparency withstand the test of time and nurture a relationship that flourishes amidst life's challenges with resilience and grace.

Your relationship will be richer with each intentional act of transparency, whether it is through opening communication about thoughts, feelings, mistakes, and aspirations; setting goals for accountability that both parties can work toward; celebrating honesty, even when it is challenging; or using tools like shared calendars or journals.

As you proceed on this journey to increase transparency in your marriage, keep in mind that each step you take will bring the two of you closer together and forge a bond based on reliability that will withstand any challenges life may present.

Moments where vulnerability and understanding, honesty and acceptance, love and resilience collide on this path to a deeper connection are all interwoven into the exquisite fabric of your life's journey together as a husband and wife who are fully dedicated to fostering a relationship overshadowed by an agape love as illustrated in 1Corinthians 13:4-7.

Chapter 11

Familial and Social Influences

NAVIGATING FAMILY EXPECTATIONS

When navigating with family expectations, it is crucial to remember that God has designed marriage to be a sacred union between a husband and a wife (Genesis 2:24). This bond is intended to be the primary relationship one that supersedes even family ties. Jesus himself recognized the importance of marital unity when He spoke about leaving one's family to establish a new household (Matthew 19:5). Family expectations, while often rooted in love, can sometimes conflict with a couple's values and goals. Prioritizing God's design for marriage is important to navigate these expectations with grace and clarity.

Family expectations can be both a source of support and a significant pressure point. Understanding these dynamics is critical in maintaining harmony within your marriage. The pressure to conform to traditional roles is a common thread when family members hold onto ideals that may not align with your modern views. This can affect everything from career choices to the division of household responsibilities.

Expectations around family planning and child-rearing often become focal points of familial pressure. Whether it is the timing of starting a family or the methods of raising children, such expectations can create strain. These pressures can lead to internal conflict and even resentment if not addressed openly and honestly. It is essential to recognize that these expectations, while rooted in love and tradition, need to be balanced with your marital values and goals.

Establishing boundaries with family members requires a balance of assertiveness and diplomacy. Family meetings can be an effective way to discuss and establish clear boundaries. Such meetings provide a platform for open dialogue, allowing each party to express needs and expectations. Alternatively, if verbal communication is difficult, writing letters to family members can be a more effective or private way to convey your boundaries and needs. Letters give you the chance to express your ideas without the pressure of immediate reactions. They can promote understanding without conflict and act as a gentle reminder of your values.

Ephesians 5:25-33 teaches that husbands are to love their wives as Christ loves the Church, providing sacrificially, while wives are to respect and support their husbands. Even in situations where outside pressures attempt to dictate roles or choices, the love and respect demonstrated in the marriage relationship should serve as the guiding principle. A happy marriage requires striking a balance between marital values and family influence. Developing a mission statement for your nucleus is an empowering testament. This statement serves as a guiding light to help you prioritize marital decisions above outside viewpoints. It reaffirms that your marriage is a distinct entity with its own set of values and goals. By focusing on what truly matters to you as a couple, you can navigate external influences with clarity and strength.

Managing conflicts with family expectations requires patience and strategic thinking. When disagreements arise, consider using mediation to resolve family disputes in a mutually amicable manner. A neutral party can facilitate discussions, ensuring that all voices are heard and respected. If tensions persist, seeking support from a family therapist may provide the necessary tools to navigate these challenges effectively. Therapy provides a safe space for exploring underlying issues and developing strategies for conflict resolution.

The goal of these techniques is to create a respectful balance where love and understanding flourish, rather than distancing oneself from family. By keeping this balance, you can benefit from the guidance and support that family provides without sacrificing the integrity of your marriage.

Family Boundary Planning

Reflect on the current familial pressures that impact your marriage. Identify specific areas where boundaries may need reinforcement or re-evaluation. Discuss with your spouse how you can establish and maintain boundaries that reflect your marriage's values while retaining healthy family relationships.

Navigating these familial expectations involves acknowledging their impact on your relationship dynamics while asserting your own values as a couple. It is about finding a way to move forward that respects both heritage and individuality while allowing your marriage to flourish amidst external influences.

Keeping the biblical framework in mind while navigating family pressures can help couples honor God's plan for their marriage and establish healthy boundaries.

Overcoming Societal Norms and Stereotypes

Societal norms often present challenges to marriage ranging from outdated gender roles to the false dichotomy between career and family life. Couples need to establish their own relationship norms to combat stereotypes and solidify the basis of the relationship. It is essential to recognize that each partner contributes in distinct ways based on unique talents and abilities. Identifying principles that matter as a couple and being able to articulate them to one another is an empowering step. Documenting these shared values and principles will guide the relationship and act as a reminder when necessary. It allows couples to determine what truly matters to them independent of external influences. Regular reviews of this document of values ensures that it evolves with the relationship, accommodating changes in circumstances and priorities. This continuous adaptation fosters a dynamic partnership that remains aligned with each spouse's growth and aspirations.

External criticism can seem like a constant presence, hovering over personal choices and decisions, particularly if you are part of a minority that has chosen to live by faith principles within your family.

Connecting with a support network of individuals who share similar values and understand your perspective can provide a buffer against societal criticism. This community offers encouragement and wisdom, reminding you that you are not alone in your choices. Practicing assertiveness in defending your relationship decisions is equally important. Being firm in your beliefs while remaining respectful to differing opinions empowers you to stand tall against unwarranted critiques.

While societal norms can exert pressure, the ultimate power lies within the relationship itself. By identifying stereotypes and choosing to forge your path, you create a marriage that resonates with authenticity and purpose.

The transformation begins with awareness, which involves recognizing the subtle ways stereotypes infiltrate your thoughts and actions. It consists of questioning assumptions and challenging the status quo. By doing so, you pave the way for a relationship that reflects genuine connection and shared values. This journey requires courage and commitment, yet the rewards are profound - a marriage characterized by authenticity and depth. In this pursuit of authenticity, couples find strength in embracing their unique identity as one to build their own traditions.

Through this lens, overcoming societal norms becomes less about fighting against external forces and more about embracing what

makes each relationship unique and special. It is about crafting a narrative that reflects shared dreams and aspirations unencumbered by external expectations.

As spouses embark on this path together, they discover newfound freedom in defining their own story, a story that celebrates unity within the marriage. This approach fosters an environment where love flourishes against all odds thus creating a legacy of empowerment and fulfillment for future generations to admire.

The journey of overcoming societal norms is one of liberation - a liberation from preconceived notions that stifle growth and authenticity within the relationship.

Addressing External Pressures with Unity

In today's interconnected world, marriages face a myriad of external pressures. Economic strains often top the list, as financial decisions become points of contention when resources are tight. Whether caused by job instability or rising costs, if not managed wisely, these pressures can erode the foundation of a relationship. Social media and reality TV add another layer of complexity that shape a false perception of how relationships should appear. The curated perfection portrayed can lead to unrealistic expectations, leaving couples feeling inadequate when comparing themselves to others. Peer pressure is also a factor that affects how couples see themselves. There is no place for "Keeping up with the Joneses" in your relationship. These outside factors can infiltrate the most private areas of marriage and sow seeds of doubt and dissatisfaction. However, the Bible guides how to navigate these challenges together. Solomon highlights the power of unity in Ecclesiastes 4:9–12, saying that "two are better than one... because if one falls, the other can help him get back up."(NIV) This verse emphasizes the importance of teamwork in overcoming external challenges.

Presenting a united front against these pressures is not only empowering but necessary for a resilient marriage. Your established values and priorities become a guiding principle in navigating these challenges. When both spouses agree on what truly matters, decisions become more transparent and more aligned with long-term goals. In public settings, practicing joint decision-making further solidifies this unity. Whether it is handling social events or financial discussions, presenting a cohesive stance reinforces the bond between you and your spouse and makes it clear to the world that you stand together.

Strengthening the marital bond against these external forces requires intentional effort and dedication. Regular couples' retreats offer a sanctuary from life's demands and provides space to reconnect and refocus. These retreats need not be extravagant; even a weekend getaway can rejuvenate your relationship. Setting aside regular private time for connection within the everyday routine is equally vital. Whether it is a quiet evening walk or shared hobbies, these moments reinforce your bond and create a buffer against external noise.

Open communication about external pressures is crucial for maintaining transparency and understanding. Holding weekly discussions allows you to explore how these influences impact your relationship. These conversations provide an opportunity to address concerns and celebrate successes in managing external challenges. Journaling as a couple offers another dimension to this practice. By documenting your responses to pressures, you create a tangible record of growth and resilience. This reflective exercise not only provides deeper understanding but also highlights patterns that may need addressing.

Through these strategies, you can cultivate a relationship that withstands the test of external pressures. It involves recognizing the influences that threaten your bond and actively working together to mitigate their impact. By presenting a united front, strengthening your connection, and maintaining open dialogue, you create a marriage that thrives amidst adversity.

Matthew 6:33 teaches us to seek first the Kingdom of God and His righteousness, and all other things will be added unto us. By keeping God at the center of the marriage, you can face financial strains, societal pressures, and other external influences with the faith and knowledge that God will provide. Presenting a united front in the face of external pressures reflects the strength and resilience that God desires for marriage.

Chapter 12

Cultivating Self-Awareness in Marriage

IMAGINE STANDING IN FRONT of a mirror that reflects your inner self - every strength, weakness, and potential, rather than your outward appearance. This is the core of self-awareness, which is essential to a thriving marriage. According to 1 Samuel 16:7, "man looks at the outward appearance, but the Lord looks at the heart."(NIV) Exploring the depths of your own psyche and developing a thorough understanding of who you are not only helps you achieve personal fulfillment but also improves relationship dynamics. It begins with evaluating one's strengths and weaknesses which illuminates paths for growth. Recognizing emotional triggers is equally vital; these triggers often dictate responses to situations that affect interactions with your spouse. By identifying these elements, you can better manage responses.

Enhancing self-awareness requires deliberate practice. Some of the tools mentioned here have been shared earlier, but understanding how to apply them in self-awareness is helpful. Keeping a daily journal to track feelings and thoughts is a valuable way to identify triggers, patterns, and areas for growth. As Psalm 139:23–24 says "Search me, O God, and know my heart; test me, and know my anxious thoughts."(NIV) See if there is any offensive way in me, and lead me in the way everlasting. Additionally, try engaging in activities that challenge personal beliefs and push boundaries that facilitate self-discovery. Another powerful tool is meditation which helps center your thoughts and cultivates a state of awareness. By dedicating even a few minutes each day to mindful meditation and focusing on what God, the Creator, said about you, you can develop a more profound understanding of your internal world and how it influences your marriage and daily reactions.

Sharing personal revelations with your spouse enhances mutual understanding. The Bible teaches that "The tongue has the power of life and death" (Proverbs 18:21), so use "I" statements to express how certain realizations affect you personally. For example, saying "I've notice I become defensive when I feel criticized" opens the door for constructive dialogue without assigning blame. This approach not only fosters empathy but also strengthens the connection between you and your spouse.

Continuous growth is fostered by establishing clear objectives that promote increased self-awareness and self-improvement. According to Proverbs 15:22, "Plans fail for lack of counsel, but with many advisers, they succeed."(NIV)

Self-Awareness Exploration

Reflect on a recent instance in which you experienced a strong emotional response. What triggered this reaction? How did you respond to it? In your journal, write about this experience and any self-discoveries you may have made. When you have open discussions, consider sharing these reflections with your spouse. Additionally, keep in mind that the Bible encourages being quick to listen and slow to speak (James 1:19), a reminder that reflection before responding can bring clarity and peace to your relationship.

A growth mindset enhances personal development within marriage. Embracing challenges as opportunities for learning transforms obstacles into steppingstones for personal development. As Philippians 4:13 assures, "I can do all this through him who gives me strength."(NIV) Viewing failures as chances for growth shifts the focus from blame to learning. Developing a growth-oriented approach involves setting joint learning goals with your spouse while encouraging each other to step out of your comfort zones. Overcoming barriers to a growth mindset requires addressing fears of failure and rejection. Proverbs 3:5-6 encourages, "Trust in the Lord with all your heart and lean not on your own understanding; in all your ways submit to him, and he will make your paths straight."(NIV) Challenging limiting beliefs about yourself and the relationship paves the way for embracing change and progress.

Practicing growth-focused reflection reinforces this mindset. Journaling about personal growth experiences provides clarity and tracks development over time. Engaging in regular self-assessments enables you to evaluate your progress and adjust your goals as needed. This practice encourages continuous learning and adaptation, essential components of a resilient marriage. As 2 Peter 3:18 encourages, "But grow in the grace and knowledge of our Lord and Savior Jesus Christ."(NIV)

Self-awareness serves as the compass on this path of introspection that guide you toward a deeper connection and fulfillment within your marriage. By understanding yourself better, you create a foundation for lasting love and harmony with your spouse.

Identifying and Changing Unhealthy Patterns

In the tapestry of marriage, specific threads can fray, leading to repetitive arguments and unresolved issues. Recognizing these detrimental habits is crucial for maintaining a healthy relationship. Hebrews 12:1 tells us, "... let us strip off every weight that slows us down, especially the sin that so easily trips us up. And let us run with endurance the race God has set before us ."(NIV) Although the issues that entangle you may not be sin, they produce cycles that hinder progress. These patterns often arise from deeply rooted behaviors and unspoken expectations that, if left unchecked, can erode the foundation of your relationship. Avoidance of difficult conversations is another typical pattern where silence serves as a protective shield against potential conflict. Yet, this silence often speaks volumes, creating distance and misunderstanding. By acknowledging these patterns, you take the first step towards change thus paving the way for healthier interactions.

Deliberate action and dedication are necessary to change these unhealthy patterns. Establishing accountability partners, whether it is a trusted friend or a therapist, can provide the support needed to initiate and sustain change. Proverbs 27:17 reminds us, "As iron sharpens iron, so one person sharpens another."(NIV) Spouses act as mirrors reflecting behaviors you may overlook. Setting clear, actionable steps for behavior modification is equally important. Instead of vague resolutions like "communicate better," focus on specific actions such as "discuss finances weekly." Patience and consistent effort are essential as you work to replace old habits with new, constructive behaviors that improve your relationship.

Regularly reviewing goals and strategies with your spouse creates a bond of teamwork and shared responsibility which includes opportunities to celebrate successes and reassess strategies that may need tweaking. Keeping a habit change journal allows you to track your journey, noting both triumphs and setbacks, which not only provides insight into patterns but also highlights progress that motivates continued effort.

Whether it is a special dinner or a weekend getaway, planning small rewards for milestones creates positive reinforcement that encourages continued effort. Celebrating success in changing patterns is essential to maintaining motivation. Sharing successes in a supportive community can also increase the joy of achievement. Connecting with others who understand the difficulties of changing habits, acts as a network of support where shared experiences foster connection and mutual celebration.

In the process of identifying and changing unhealthy patterns, self-awareness remains pivotal. The ability to recognize when you are slipping back into old habits allows you to course-correct before issues escalate. It is about being present and mindful in your interactions and catching yourself when you default to unproductive behaviors. This awareness invokes you to make conscious choices that align with your relationship goals. As you develop new patterns, you will likely notice a shift not only in your interactions but also in your overall relationship satisfaction.

Building new neural pathways that support positive behaviors and dismantling those that no longer serve you or your marriage is the process of continuously moving toward healthier patterns, which takes time and patience but yields a profoundly stronger connection, increased understanding, and a more harmonious relationship.

Creating a chart that displays your progress, serves as a tangible reminder of your efforts and affirms your commitment to growth. Sharing this journey with your spouse not only enhances your relationship but also reaffirms your shared vision for the future.

As you proceed on this journey of transformation, keep in mind that failures are typical and a necessary part of the process; they provide insightful lessons that help you grow and become more resilient. You should welcome them as chances to improve your tactics and to gain a deeper understanding of one another. With persistence and support from one another, you will discover that changing negative patterns into healthy ones not only enhances your relationship but also improves your personal well-being.

Regular self-assessments further enhance this process by providing structured opportunities to evaluate progress. These assessments help identify areas for growth and areas that need improvement, thus guiding the setting of future goals. Through self-reflection, you gain a greater understanding of your journey, enabling you to appreciate the progress made and identify new directions for growth.

The Role of Self-Care in a Healthy Marriage

Self-care, often misunderstood as a form of indulgence, is essential to maintaining a healthy marriage. It includes taking intentional and respectful care of one's spiritual, physical, emotional, and mental well-being. It is not just about personal gain but also benefits the relationship by preventing burnout and boosting resilience. When you take care of yourself, you bring a balanced, rejuvenated self to your relationship, which forms the foundation of a marriage that can withstand life's pressures. Without self-care, stress builds up, leading to fatigue and irritability, which depletes the energy needed to maintain the relationship thus creating a vicious cycle of neglect and discontent.

In 1 Corinthians 6:19-20, Paul reminds us that our bodies are temples of the Holy Spirit; therefore, we must honor God through them. Incorporating self-care into daily life ensures that both spouses remain balanced and fulfilled. It does not require grand gestures. It begins with small, intentional actions that honor your well-being. Simple practices such as setting aside time for hobbies, a hot bath, an evening walk or spending time with friends, promote creativity and joy. This time is a sacred commitment to yourself that enhances your ability to fully engage with your spouse.

Gratitude and positive affirmations help you shift your focus from what is lacking to what is abundant therefore creating a mindset of appreciation and contentment. These affirmations are gentle reminders of your value and the blessings in your marriage.

The marital bond is strengthened when both spouses support each other's self-care endeavors. Promoting personal hobbies and relaxation, while acknowledging the value of personal space for overall well-being, aligns with Philippians 2:4: "Let each of you look not only to his own interests but also to the interests of others."(NIV) Partaking in self-care activities can also strengthen bonds by offering chances for shared experiences that benefit both parties.

Encouraging your spouse to pursue hobbies or leisure activities shows respect for individuality and creates an atmosphere where both feel appreciated and understood. Sharing self-care activities, such as working out together or spending a peaceful evening at home, enriches connection and strengthens intimacy while reaffirming the value of balanced care in the relationship.

Developing a customized self-care plan aligns with both individual and collective needs. Start by identifying the activities you enjoy, such as reading, gardening, or fishing. Ensuring it is realistic and achievable, adjust your plan to suit your lifestyle. Having attainable self-care goals gives you focus and drive and turn dreams into actionable steps. This plan serves as a roadmap that guides you toward a balanced life that respects both your personal health and marital harmony.

Discussing self-care priorities regularly helps resolve conflicts that may arise between individual desires and shared responsibilities. It takes intentionality and commitment on the part of both spouses to integrate self-care into daily routines. Recognizing the importance of balance in life and making conscious choices that support well-being produce long term benefits. This commitment transforms self-care from an occasional indulgence into an integral part of daily life.

As you integrate these practices into your marriage, remember that self-care is not a selfish act, but rather essential for sustaining love of self and others. It empowers you to bring your best self into the relationship as you navigate life together.

Conclusion

As we reach the end of **Marriage Respiced**, I want to remind you of the vision that has guided us throughout this journey. I have aimed to restore the sacred view of marriage by revisiting God's original design - a design rooted in love, commitment, and covenant. It is a vision that calls us to see marriage not merely as a contract, but as a divine covenant that mirrors God's unwavering love and dedication to His people.

Throughout this book, we have explored various themes essential to nurturing a Christ-centered marriage. We began with the divine blueprint of marriage, understanding it as a reflection of the relationship between God and humanity. We then explored building a Christ-centered marriage emphasizing the importance of communication, emotional intimacy, and navigating conflict with grace. Each chapter has provided a roadmap to strengthen your union and rekindle physical intimacy.

As you reflect on these themes, consider the key takeaways that can transform your marriage. Embrace active listening and empathy to deepen your communication. Foster emotional and physical intimacy as expressions of love and connection. Remember that passionate sex is not a sin but a celebration of God's amazing gift to marriage. Approach conflicts as opportunities for growth and healing. Cultivate a shared financial vision and support each other's dreams. Embrace your individuality while nurturing your relationship. Above all, seek to embody the love, grace, and patience that Christ demonstrates for His Church.

I encourage you to take these insights and apply them to your marriage. Let them guide you as you navigate the complexities and joys of your union. Reflect on the exercises and practices shared throughout the book. Use them as tools to enhance your relationship, whether through prayer, open dialogue, or shared activities. Remember, the journey toward a thriving marriage is continuous and requires intentionality and commitment.

Take specific steps daily towards enriching your marriage. Schedule regular times for prayer, worship and reflection with your spouse. Set aside moments to express gratitude and affirm each other's strengths. Create routines that celebrate your values and dreams. Engage in meaningful conversations that build connection and understanding. Let your marriage be a testament to God's love, and by your example an inspiration for others.

I am deeply grateful for the opportunity to share this journey with you. Your commitment to strengthening your marriage reflects a profound dedication to love and faith. I am honored to have been a part of this transformative process. I hope the insights shared in this book will continue to support and inspire you as you build a marriage grounded on God's principles.

As you move forward, embrace the sacredness of your marriage. Let it shine as a beacon of hope and love, grounded in the divine blueprint that God has designed. May your union thrive in every season of life, reflecting His grace and commitment. Remember, you are not alone on this journey. Embrace the love and support of family and friends, knowing that God's ears are always open to His children's prayers. With faith, love, and perseverance, your marriage can flourish becoming a source of joy, strength, and stability for generations to come.

May your marriage be a living testament to the beauty and power of a Christ-centered union. Embrace the journey ahead with hope and excitement knowing that God's love and guidance are with you every step of the way.

Prayer: Father, as couples embark on this journey to renew their marriage covenant, help them to see each other through Your eyes. Teach them the true meaning of Agape love. Help them to love unselfishly, forgive continually, and honor You with every decision they make. May their love grow and their intimacy flourish daily as they draw closer to You and to one another. In Jesus' Name, Amen.

References

- *Ancient Jewish Wedding Customs and Yeshua's Second ...* https://www.messianicbible.com/feature/ancient-jewish-wedding-customs-and-yeshuas-second-coming/

- Betrayal. (n.d.). In *Merriam-Webster.com dictionary.* Retrieved [June 25, 2025], from https://www.merriam-webster.com/dictionary/betrayal

- *The Challenges of Intercultural Marriages| Interpersonal* https://interpersona.psychopen.eu/index.php/interpersona/article/view/8047/8047.html

- *Consequences of Betrayal Trauma in Marriage - Karuna Healing* https://karunahealing.org/consequences-of-betrayal-trauma-in-marriage/Dweck, C.S. (2006). *Mindset: The New Psychology of Success.* Random House

- *Genesis 2—The Foundation of Marriage* https://answersingenesis.org/blogs/simon-turpin/2016/04/04/genesis-2-foundation-marriage/

- Guo, H., et al. (2019). *Hormonal Regulation of Female Reproductive Health. Endocrine Reviews, 40*(6), 1351-1365.

- *Holy Bible: New living translation.* (2015). Tyndale House Publishers.

- *Holy Bible: New international version.* (1996). Tyndale House Publishers.

- *Holy Bible: King James version.* (2020). Thomas Nelson.

- Lyndon B. Johnson Quotes. (n.d.). BrainyQuote.com. Retrieved September 01, 2025, from BrainyQuote.com https://www.brainyquote.com/quotes/lyndon_b_johnson_137074

- *Empathy In Marriage: The Secret To Thriving Relationships* https://www.sdrelationshipplace.com/empathy-in-marriage-secret-to-thriving-relationships/

- *Jewish wedding symbols - Danny Azoulay* https://ketubahazoulayart.com/jewish-wedding-symbols/

- *Under the Huppah: The Jewish Wedding* https://pluralism.org/under-the-huppah-the-jewish-wedding

- O'Connell He, Sanjeevan Kv, Hutson Jm. *Anatomy of the Clitoris.* Journal of Urology [internet]. 2005 Oct 1 [cited 2025 Aug 16];174(4 part 1):1189-95.

- *Stewarding Finances as a Christian Couple* https://www.eaglefamily.org/stewarding-finances-as-a-christian-couple/

Nuggets

BELOW ARE NUGGETS I have gathered in years of counseling couples that can help strengthen the marital connection.

Men

- If you lead her with loving hands and kind words, she will follow you wherever you go. If you lead her with angry words of disdain, you will have to drag her the whole way.

- If you treat her as your queen, she will rise to the occasion. If you treat her as your child, she will despise you.

- If you don't say it to her, someone else will.

- Quantity time that has no quality produces little fruit. She wants your attention.

- She doesn't always need you to understand it; sometimes she just wants you to do it because it makes her happy.

Women

- God gave men an ego. Build it and it will benefit you in many ways.

- Your husband wants to feel like he is your hero.

- Home is where your husband comes to feel safe from the world's expectations.

- Affirmation is important. When you tear him down with your words, you tear down your house.

- Sex is important to your husband. It is not always about intimacy. It is sometimes about a release – a way to expel all the pent-up energy from the world around him in a warm, safe space.

- Most men are logical, and it has to make sense to them.

Your spouse needs to hear you say, "I Love You", not religiously, but purposefully.

Speak to your spouse as you would speak to others outside the home whom you respect.

Your spouse observes how you interact with and attend to others, in comparison to how you interact with and attend to them.

Demonstrate to your spouse how to be the person you want him/her to be to you.

Just because *you* do not think it is broken, it does not mean it does not need to be fixed.

Keep:

1. *God first*   2. Loving   3. Learning   4. Laughing

Covenant Commitment Statement

YOU MAY CHOOSE TO read this aloud together or return to it during moments when your marriage needs realignment.

We choose to honor our marriage as a sacred covenant before God. We commit to love with intention, forgive with humility, communicate with grace, and pursue unity with faith. We acknowledge that our marriage reflects Christ and His Church, and we choose to steward this gift with reverence and devotion. With God's help, we will continue to grow together.

A Final Word

MARRIAGE WAS NEVER MEANT to be endured, it was meant to be stewarded.

As you close this book, you have been invited to see marriage not as a contract sustained by convenience, but as a **covenant upheld by faithfulness, sacrifice, and grace**. From Genesis to Revelation, Scripture reveals that marriage is a divine picture—one that reflects God's unwavering commitment to His people and Christ's sacrificial love for His Bride.

The journey you have embarked on is not about perfection. It is about **alignment**. Alignment with God's heart. Alignment with His design. Alignment with His redemptive power at work in your union.

Every healthy marriage will experience seasons of joy and sorrow, closeness and distance, abundance and stretching. What sustains a marriage through every season is not emotion, but covenant love: agape love that chooses faithfulness even when feelings waiver and appearances diminish.

If there is one truth to carry forward, let it be this: **God is not finished with your marriage.**

About the Author

SHARON FINNEY IS A Licensed Marriage and Family Therapist (LMFT) with decades of experience guiding couples through the complex realities of marriage. A devoted follower of Jesus Christ, she is passionate about helping couples build lasting, Christ-centered unions that reflect God's love, grace, and faithfulness. Her work is distinguished by its unique blend of sound therapeutic insights and deep theological grounding, offering couples a path to transformation that goes beyond quick fixes to address the heart of their relationship. She is the author of the Couples Prayer Journal for Husbands, Couples Prayer Journal for Wives, The Marriage Respiced Workbook and *Light the Fire: Flirting After I Do*. Sharon continues her mission to strengthen marriages for every season of life through counseling, marriage seminars and workshops. For more information or to schedule for your church or an event email info@marriagerespiced.com.

www.ingramcontent.com/pod-product-compliance
Lightning Source LLC
Chambersburg PA
CBHW070122100426
42744CB00010B/1902